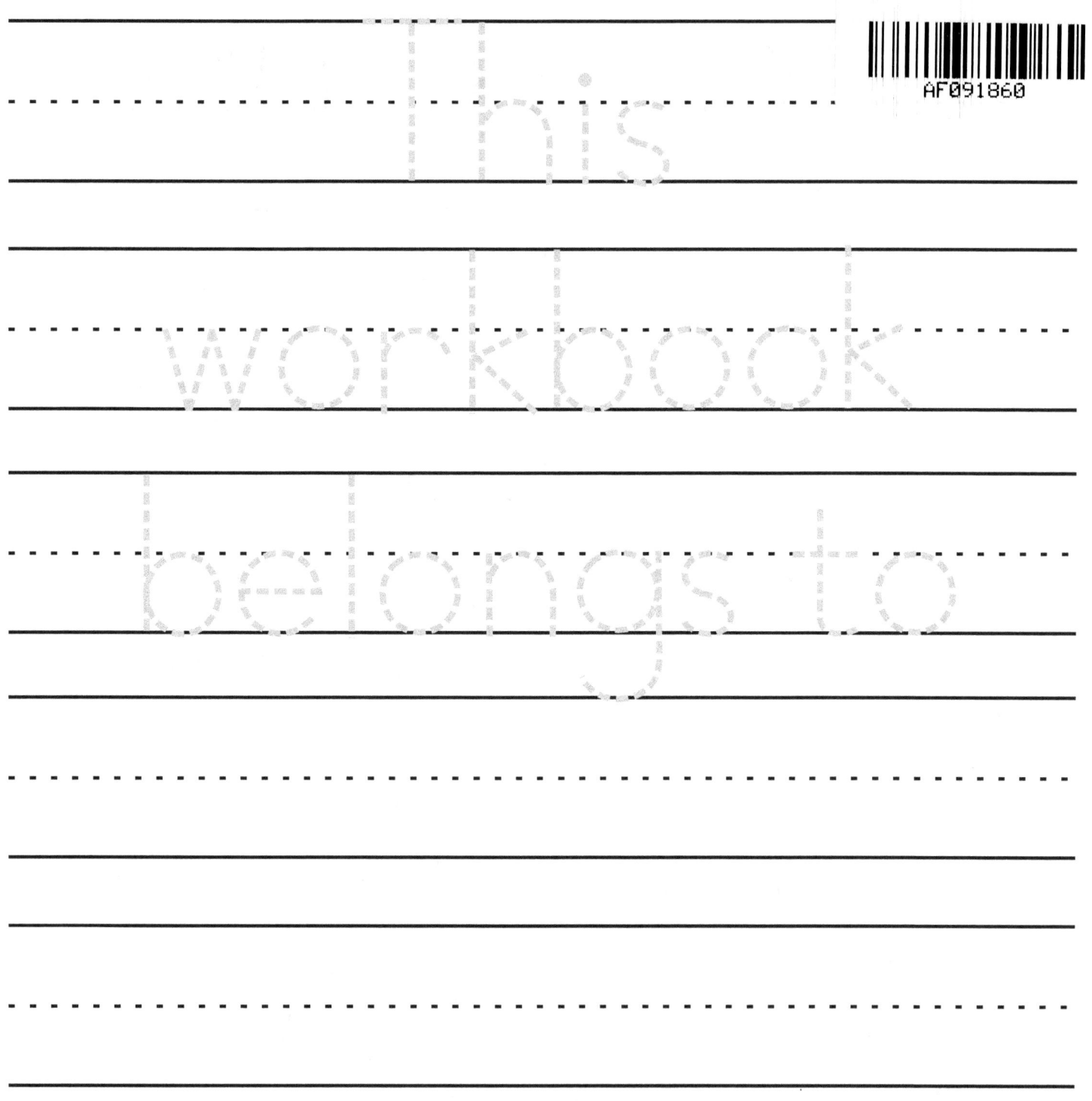

This workbook belongs to

© 2024 Life Style Daily. All rights reserved.

No part of this publication may be reproduced, distributed, or transmitted in any form or by any means, including photocopying, recording, or other electronic or mechanical methods, without the prior written permission of the publisher, except in the case of brief quotations embodied in critical reviews and certain other noncommercial uses permitted by copyright law. For permission requests, write to the publisher, addressed "Attention: Permissions Coordinator," at the address provided by Life Style Daily.

Unauthorized use and/or duplication of this material without express and written permission from Life Style Daily is strictly prohibited. Violators will be prosecuted to the fullest extent of the law.

TRACE THE LINE

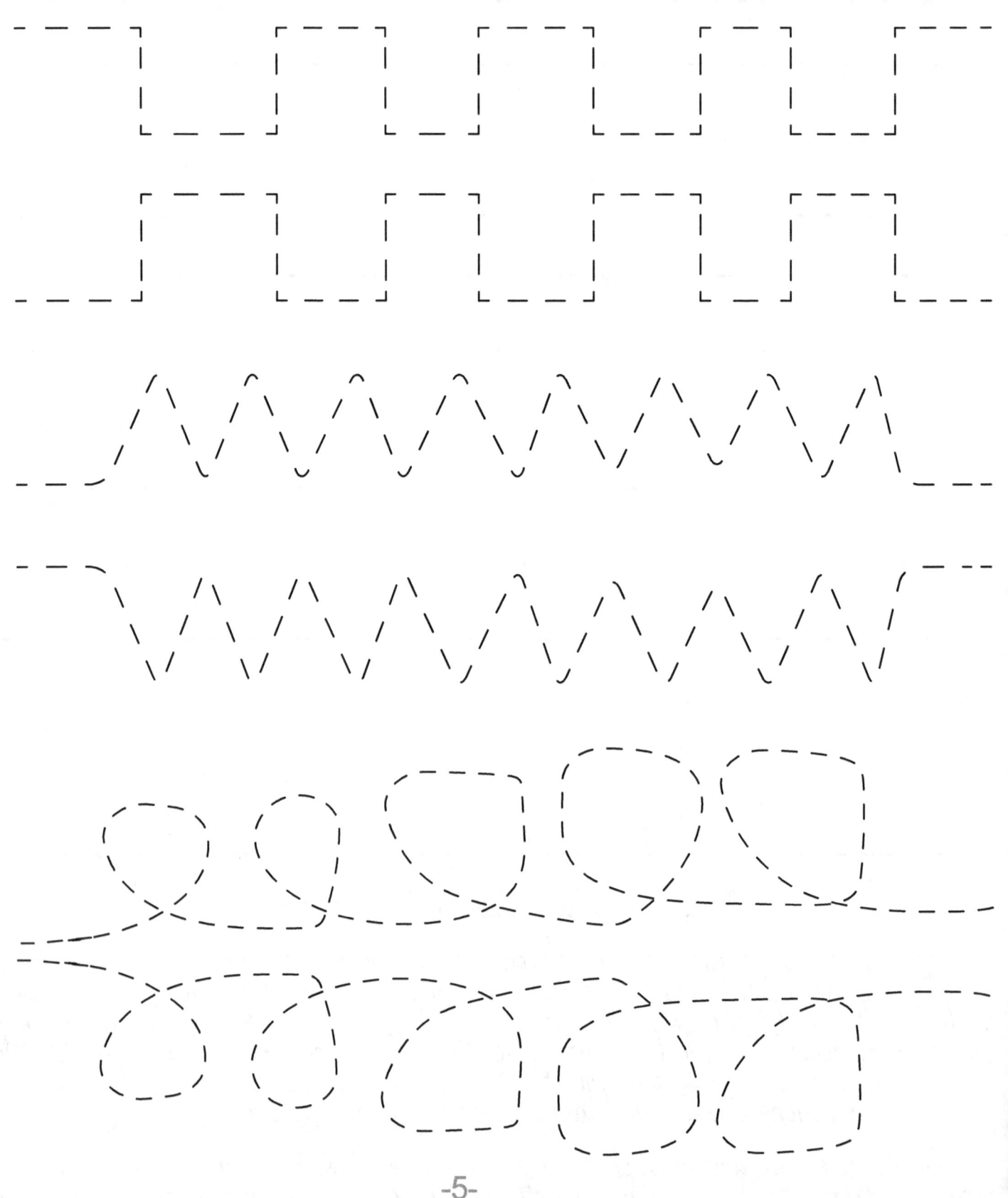

TRACE THE LINE

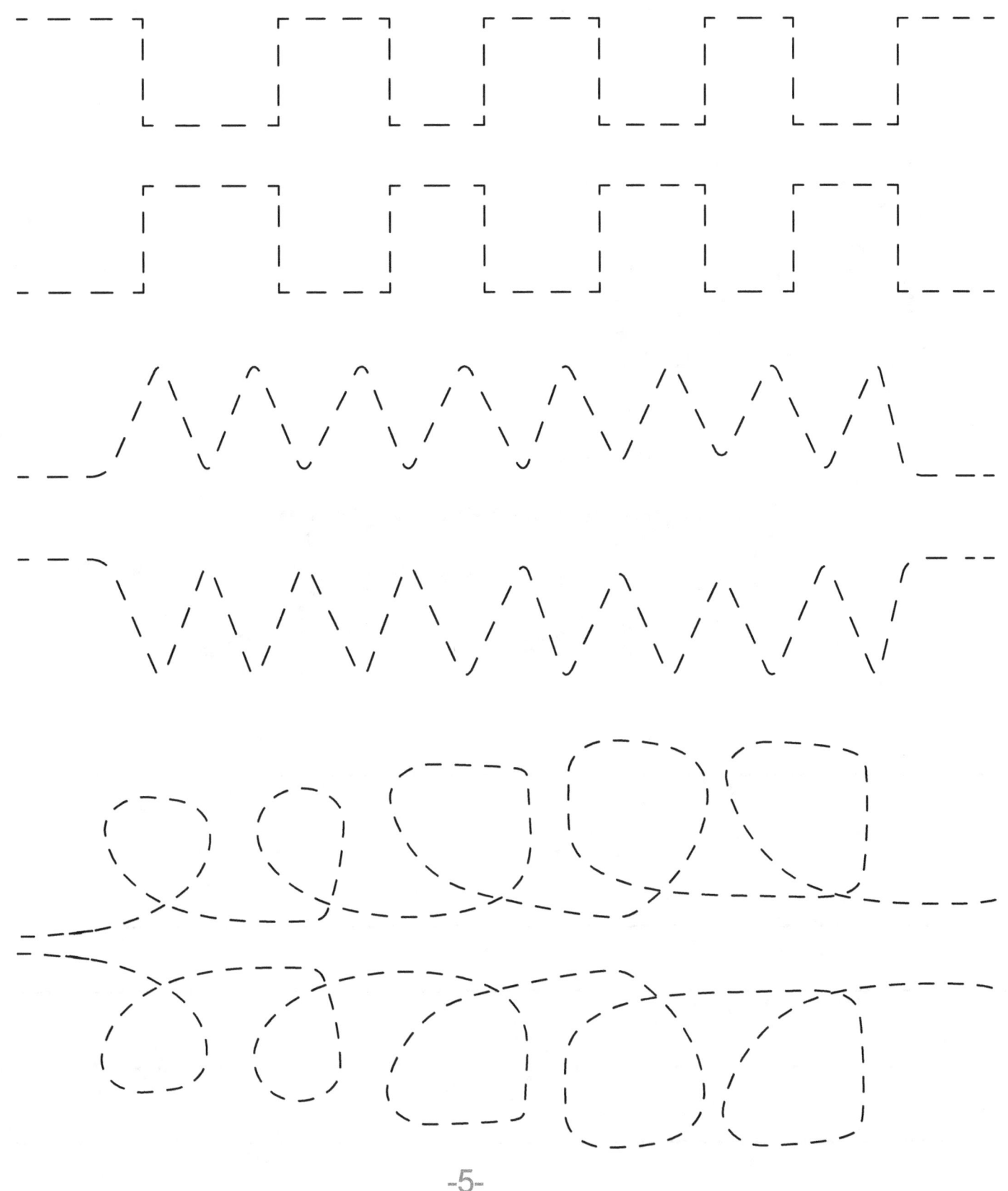

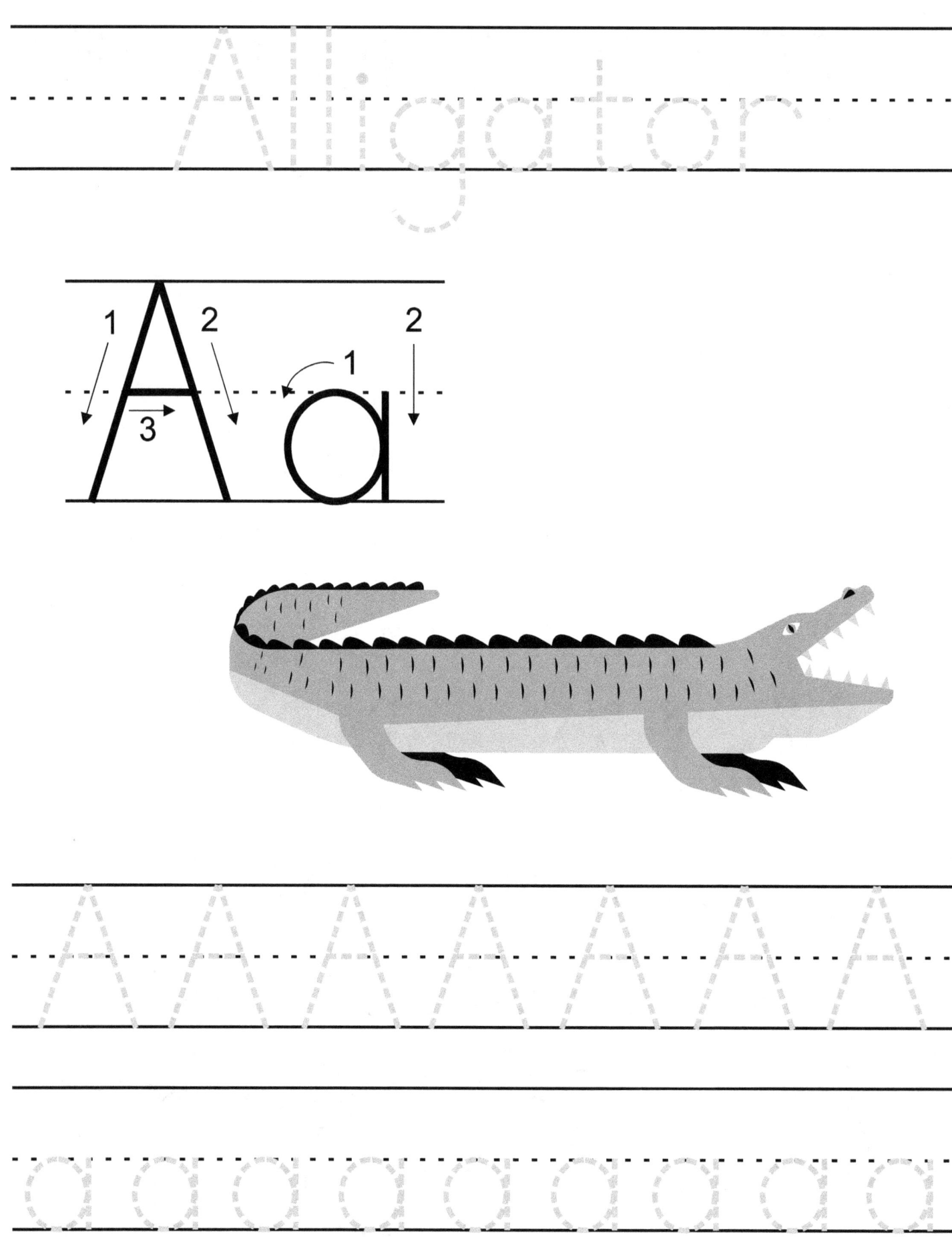

5

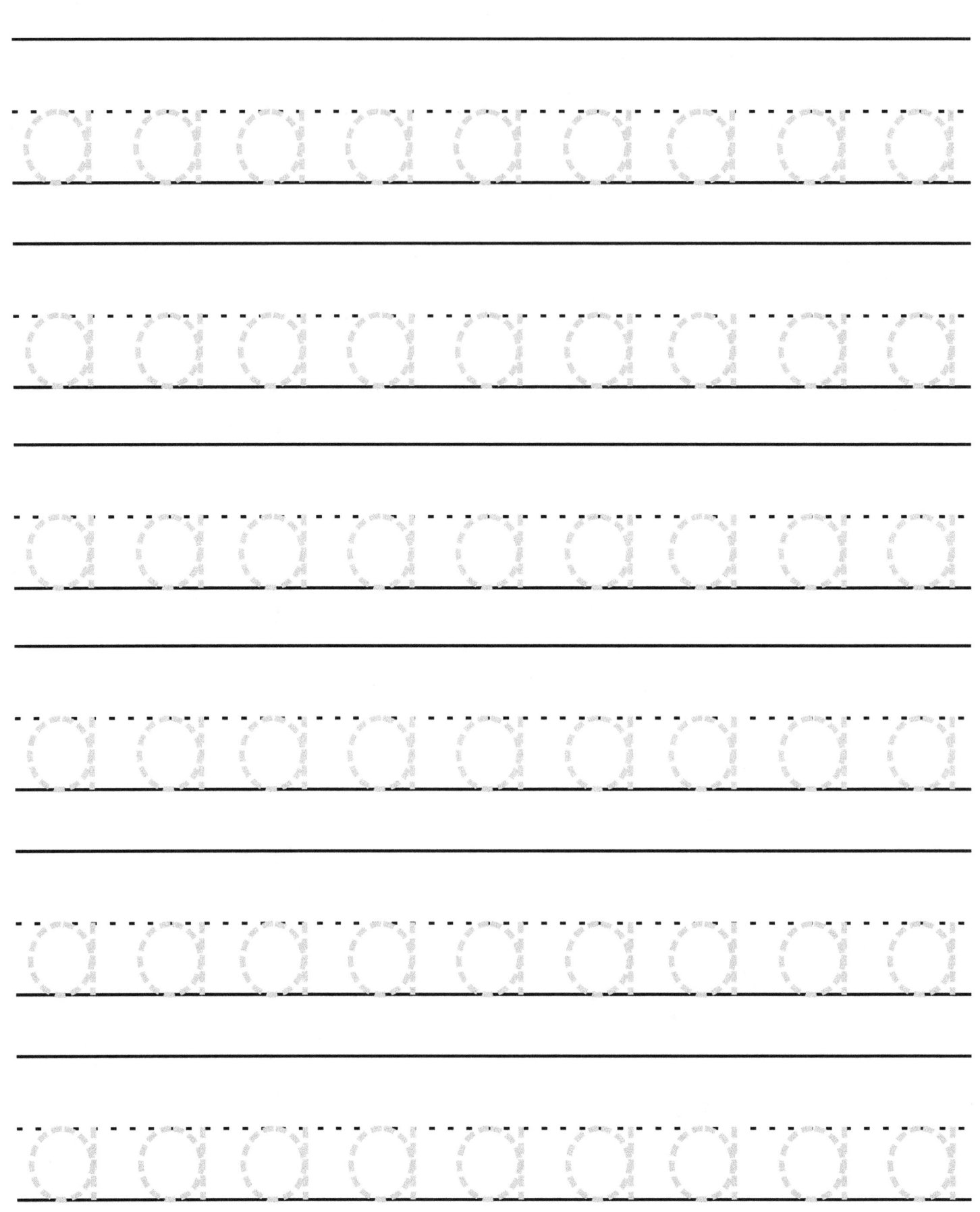

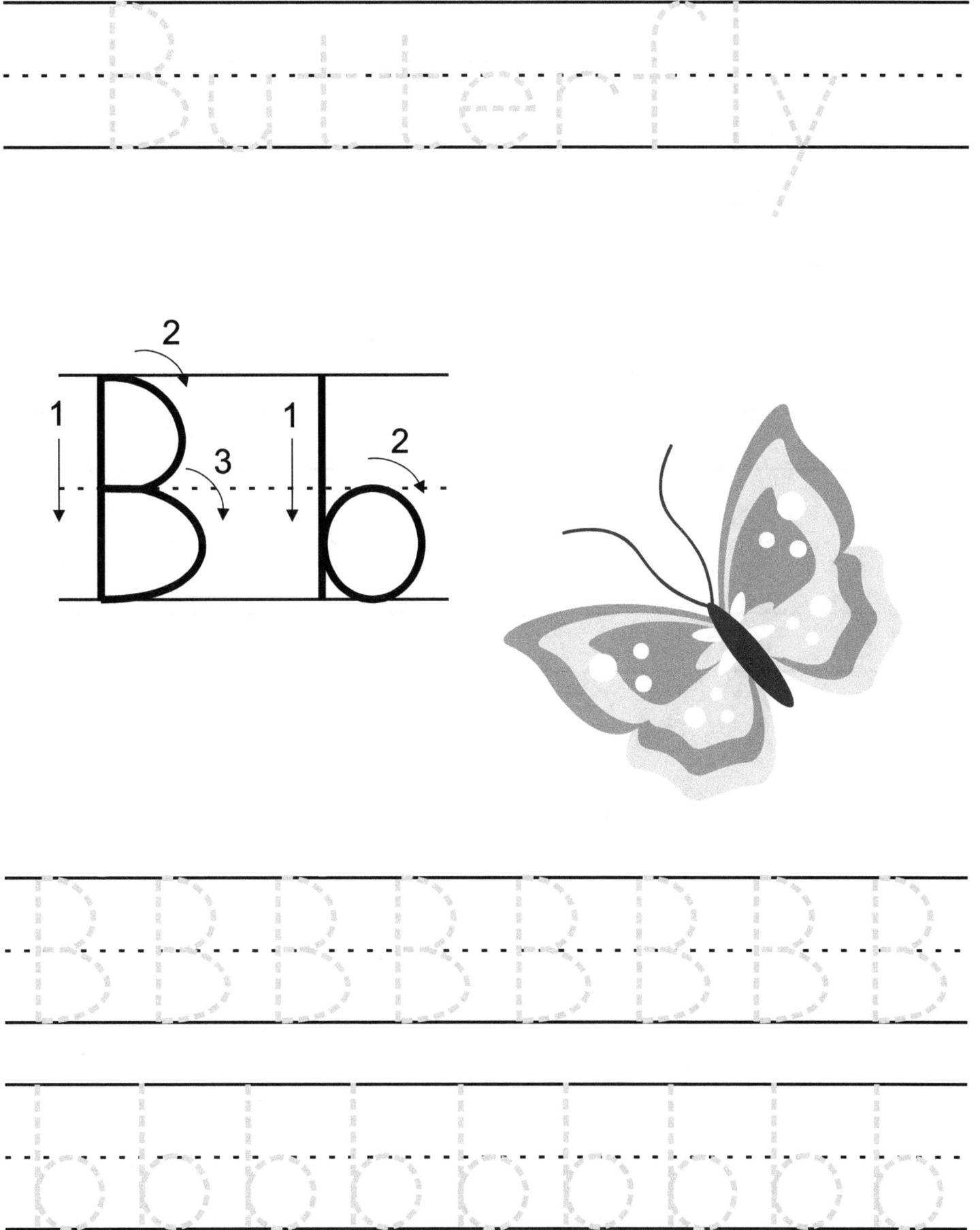

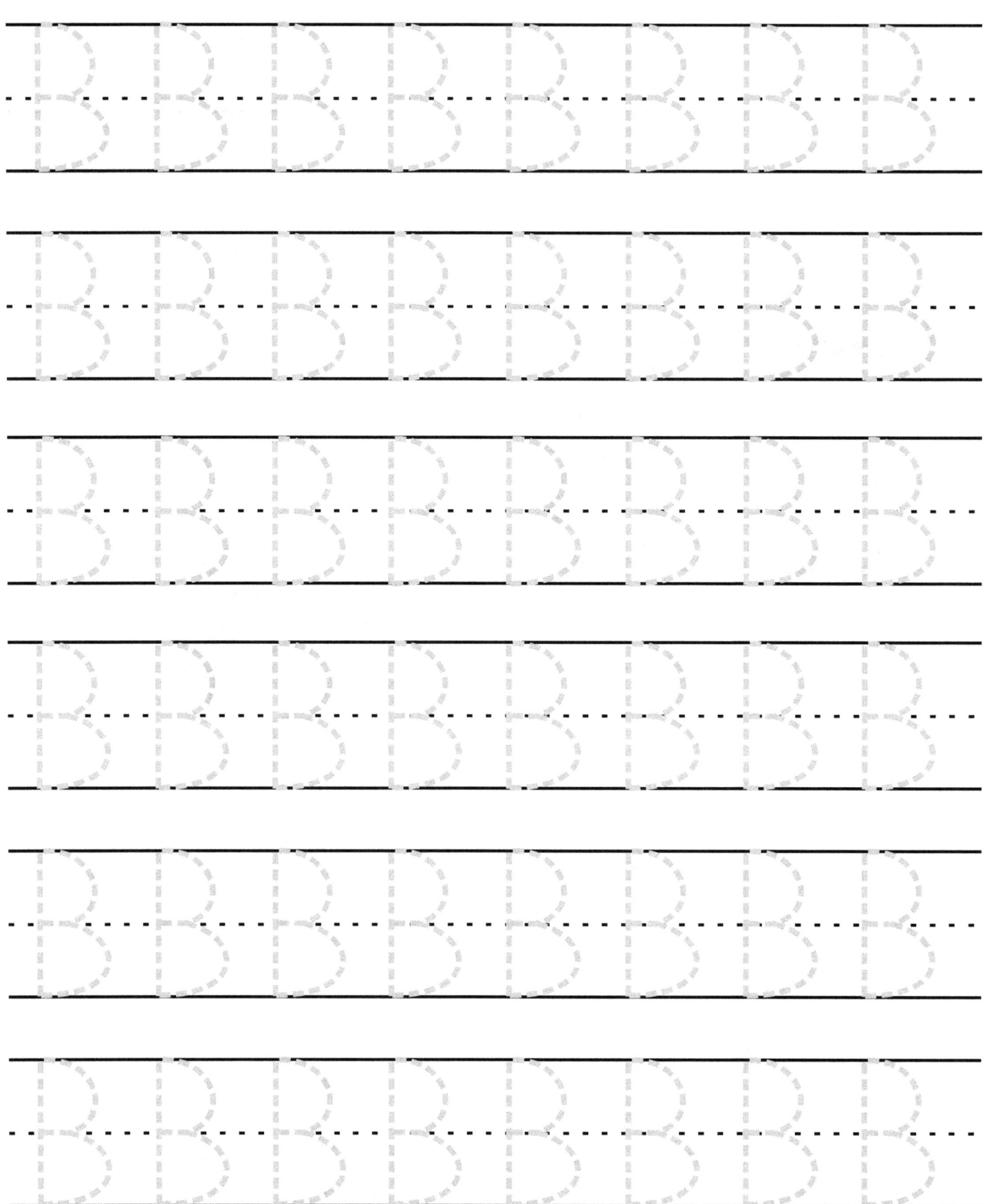

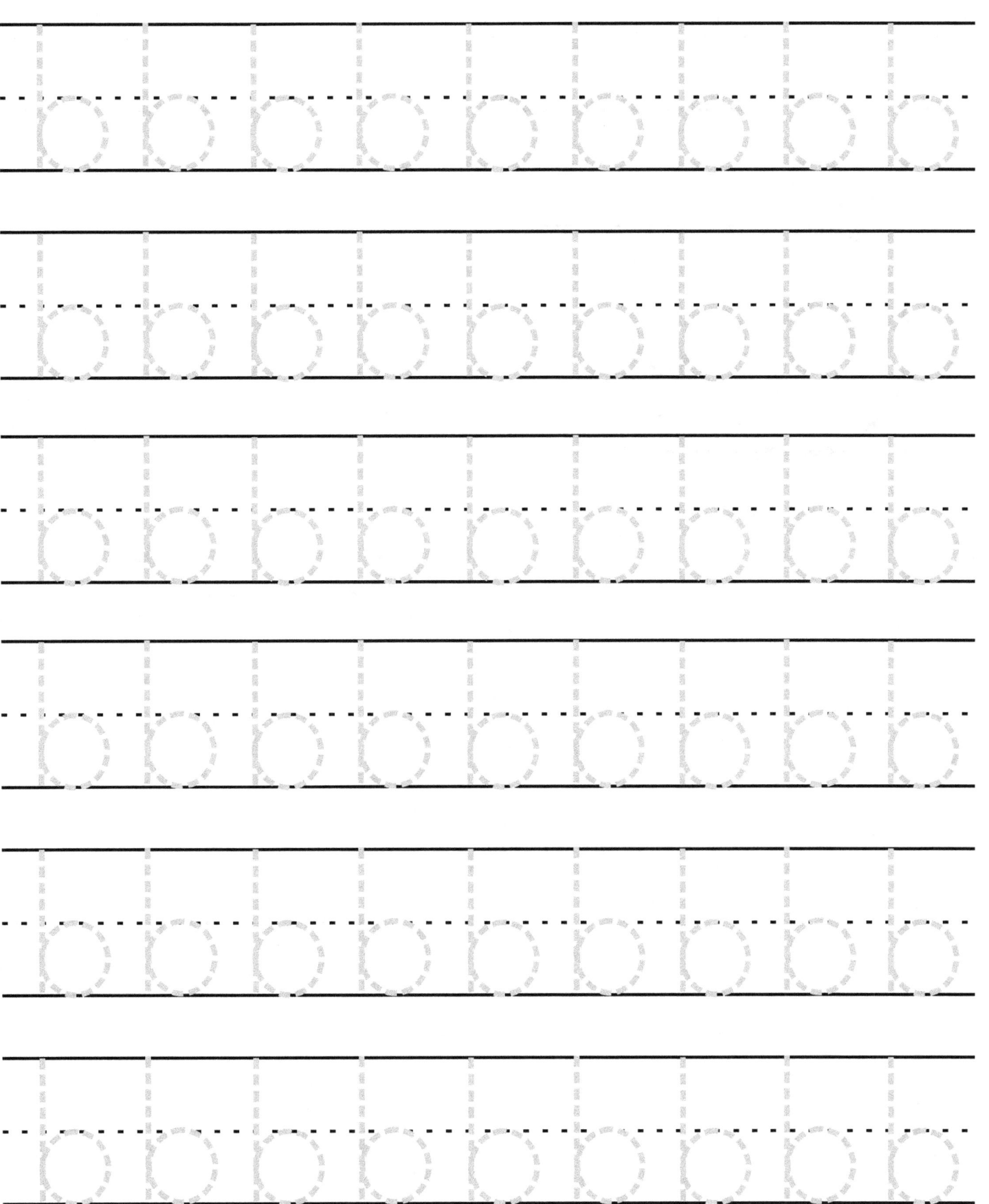

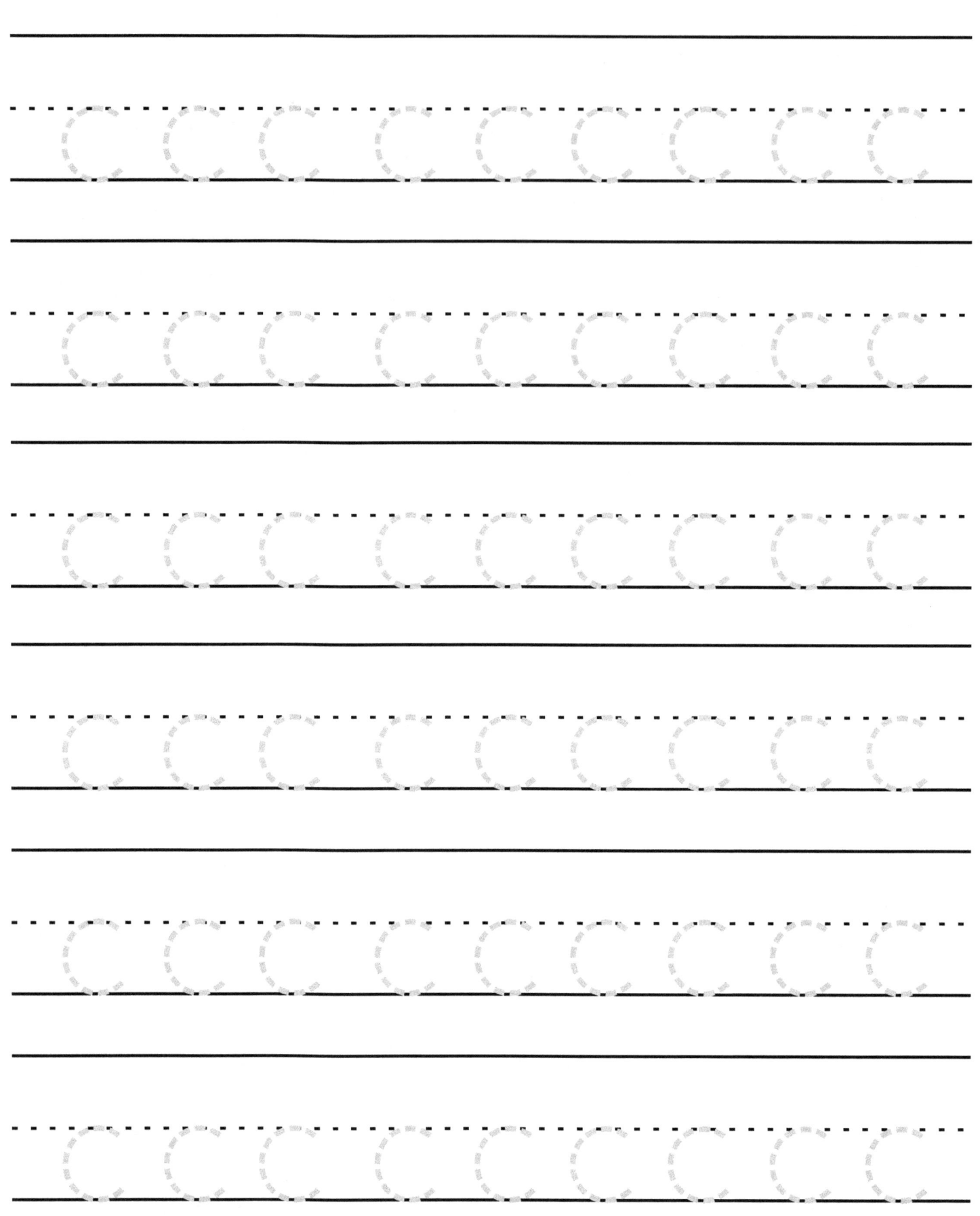

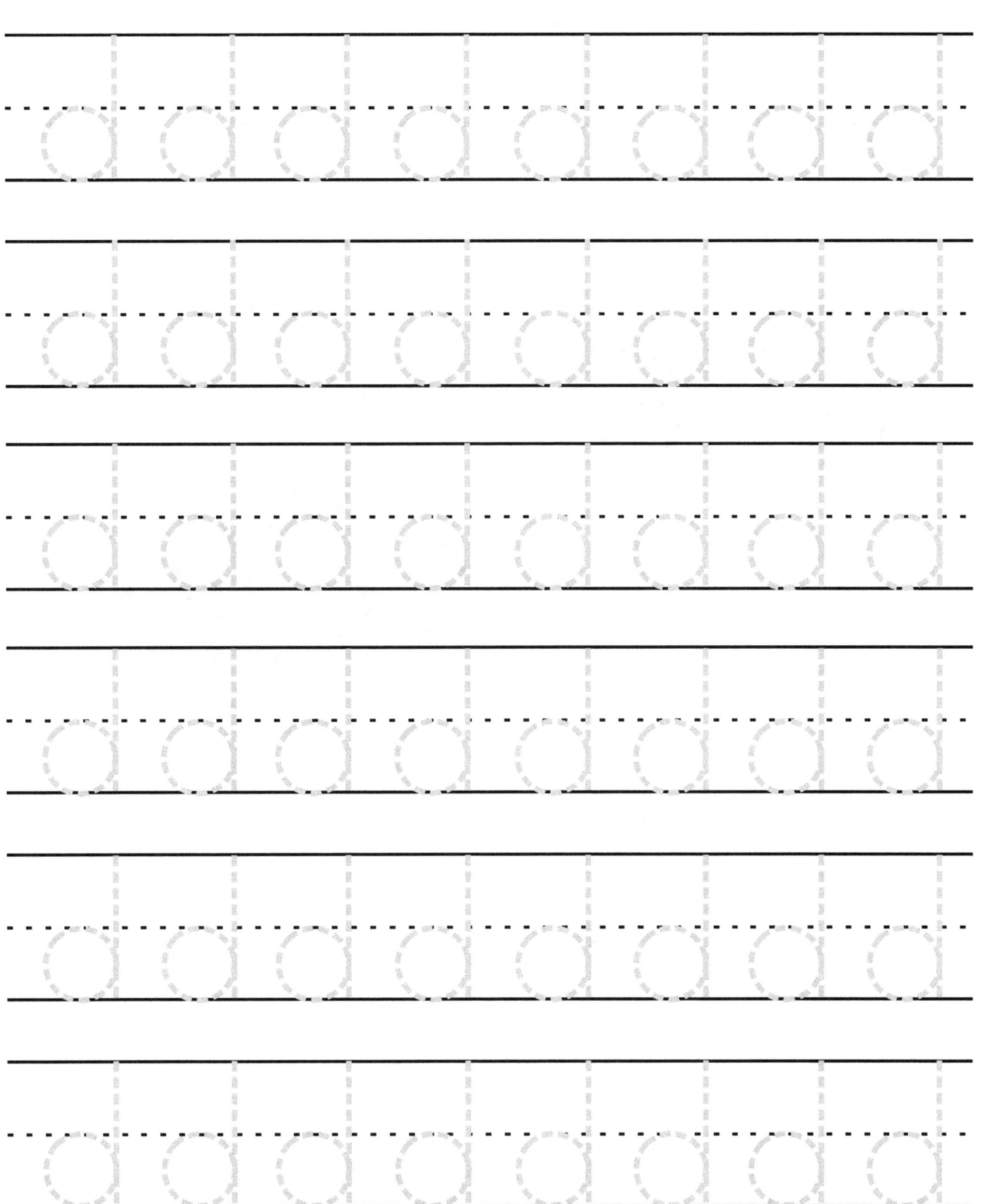

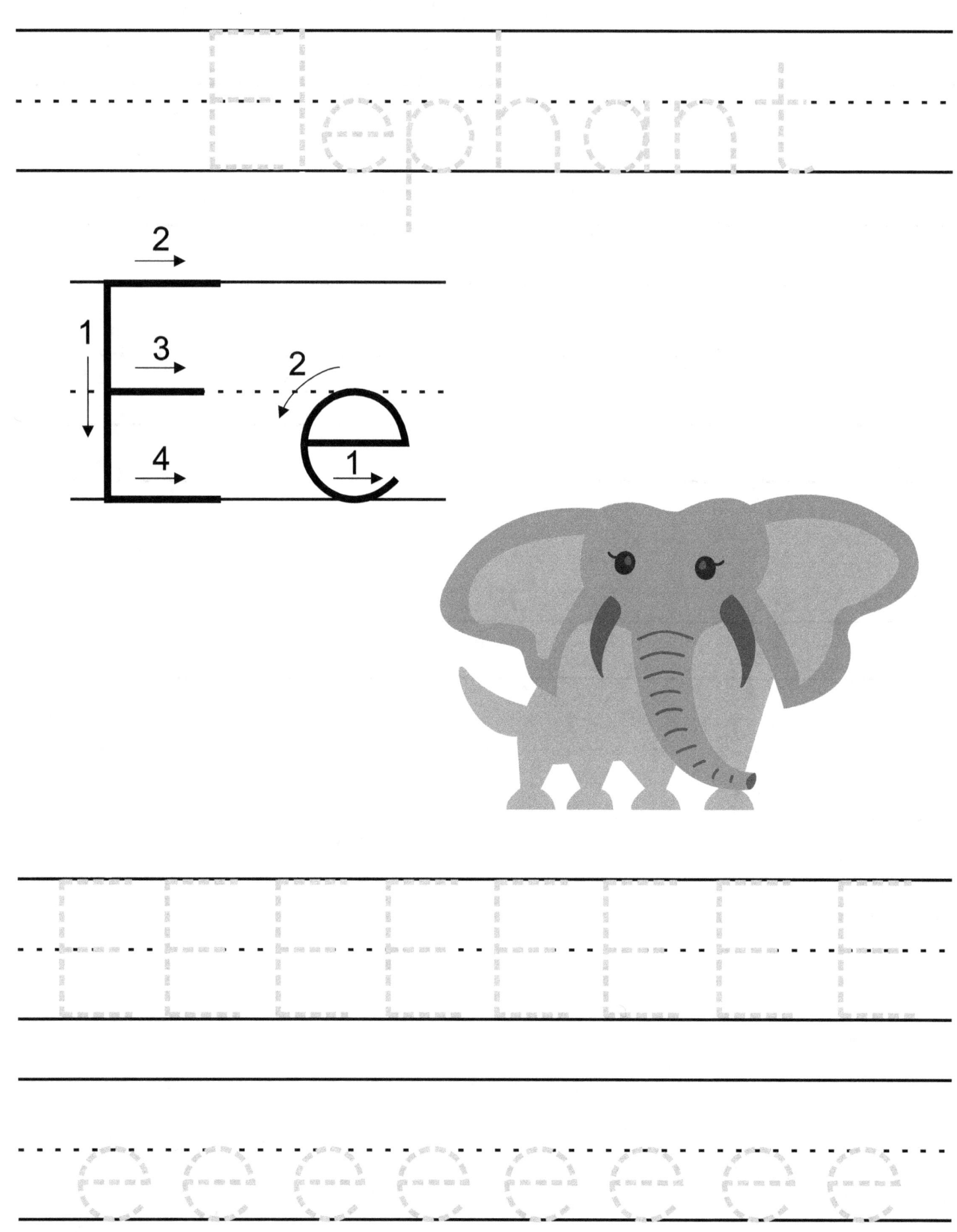

17

eeeeeeee

eeeeeeee

eeeeeeee

eeeeeeee

eeeeeeee

eeeeeeee

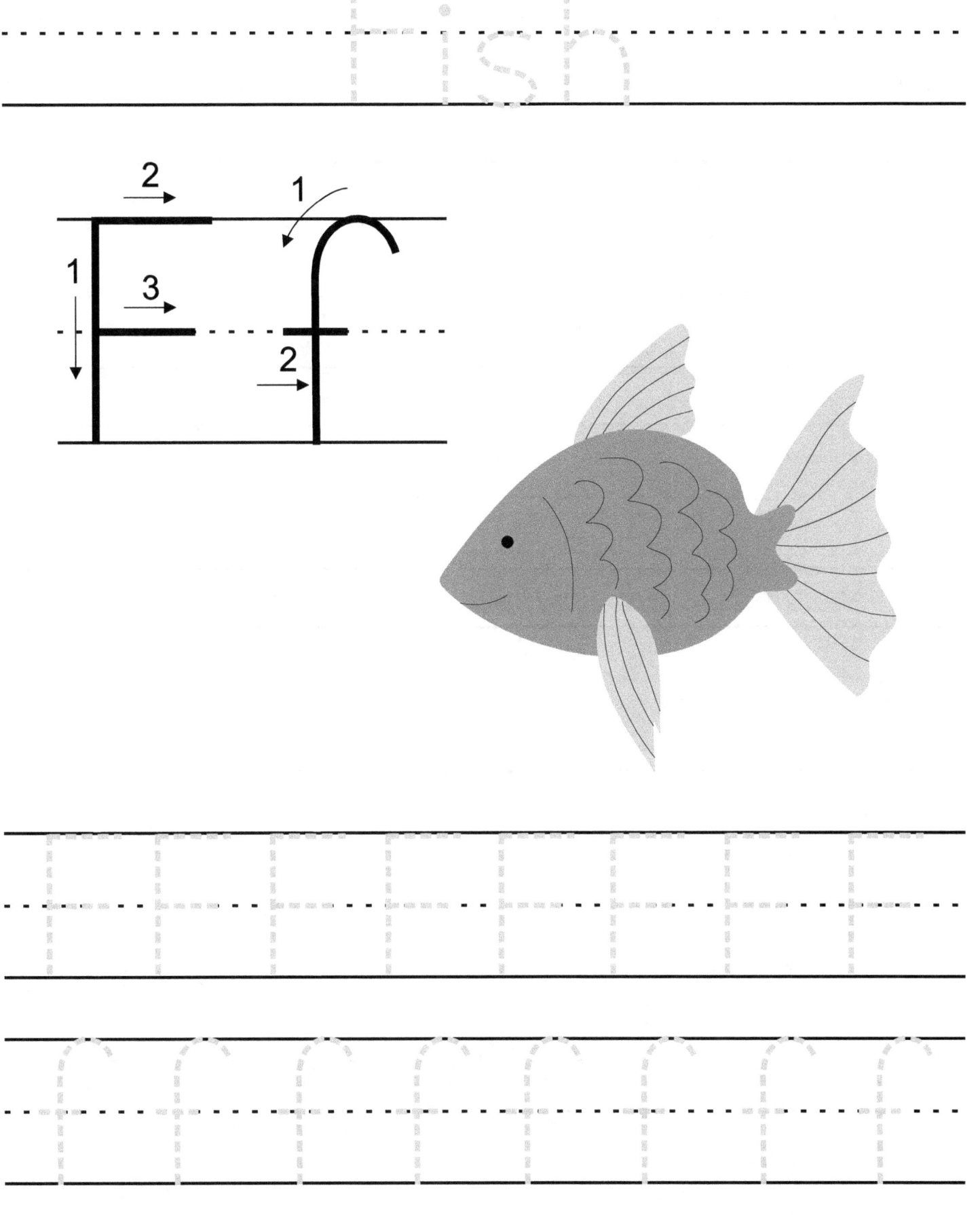

20

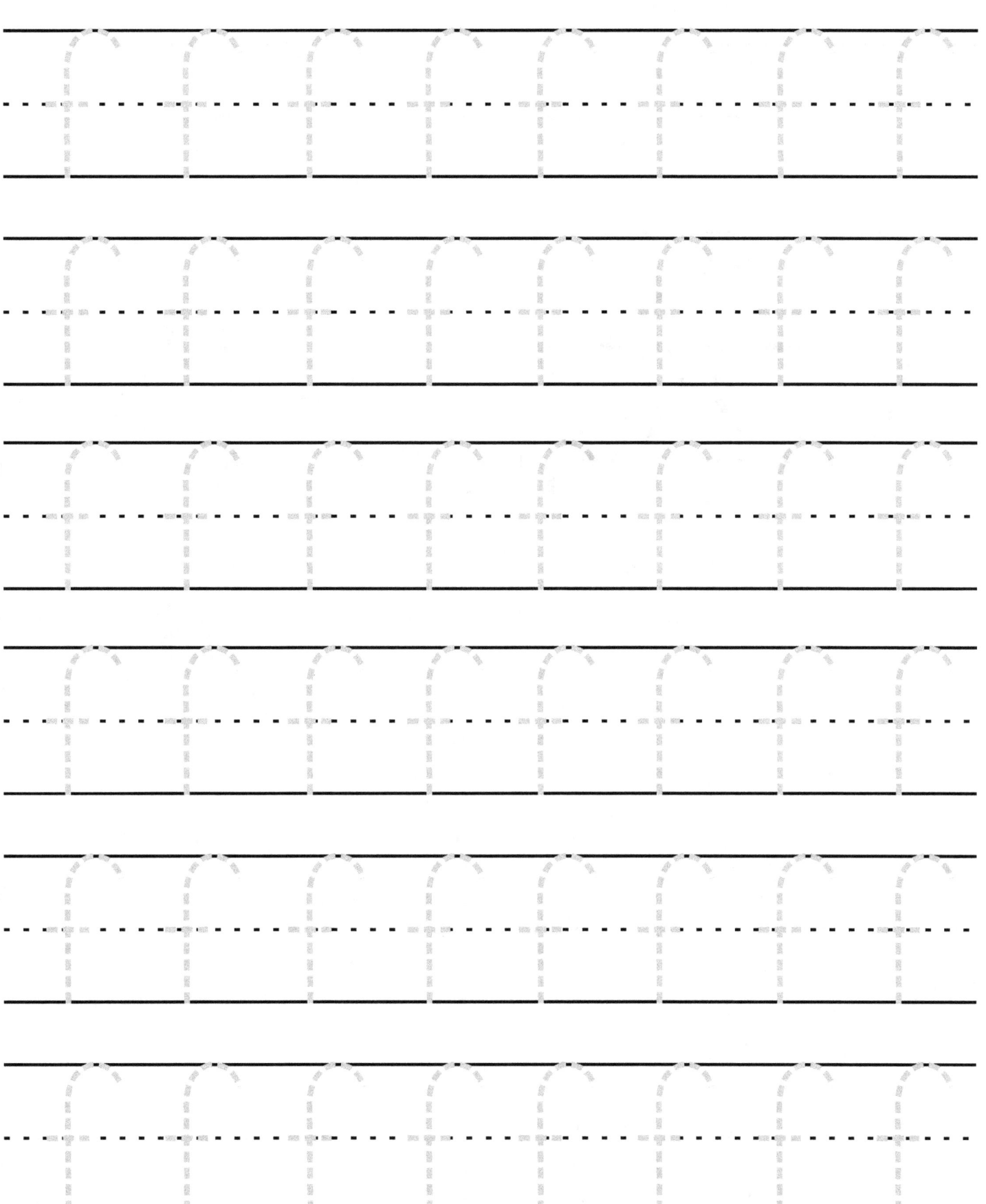

Gift

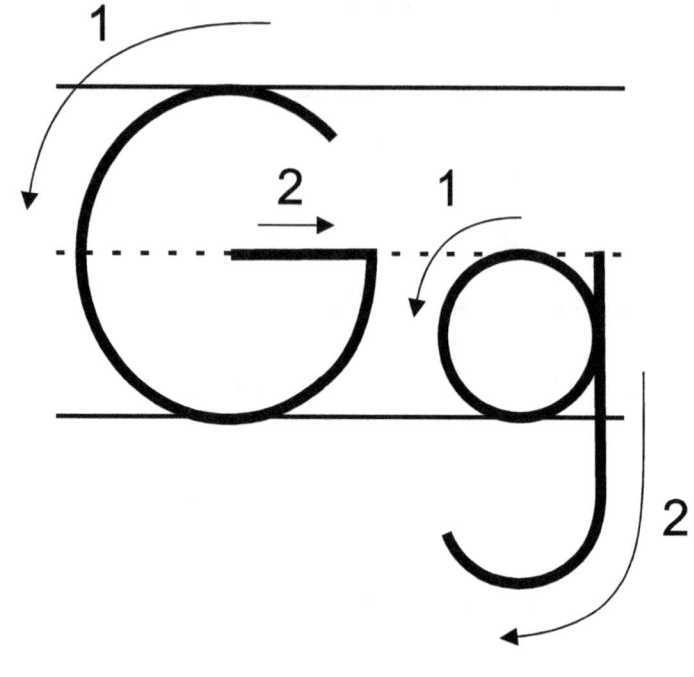

G g g g g

g g g g g g g

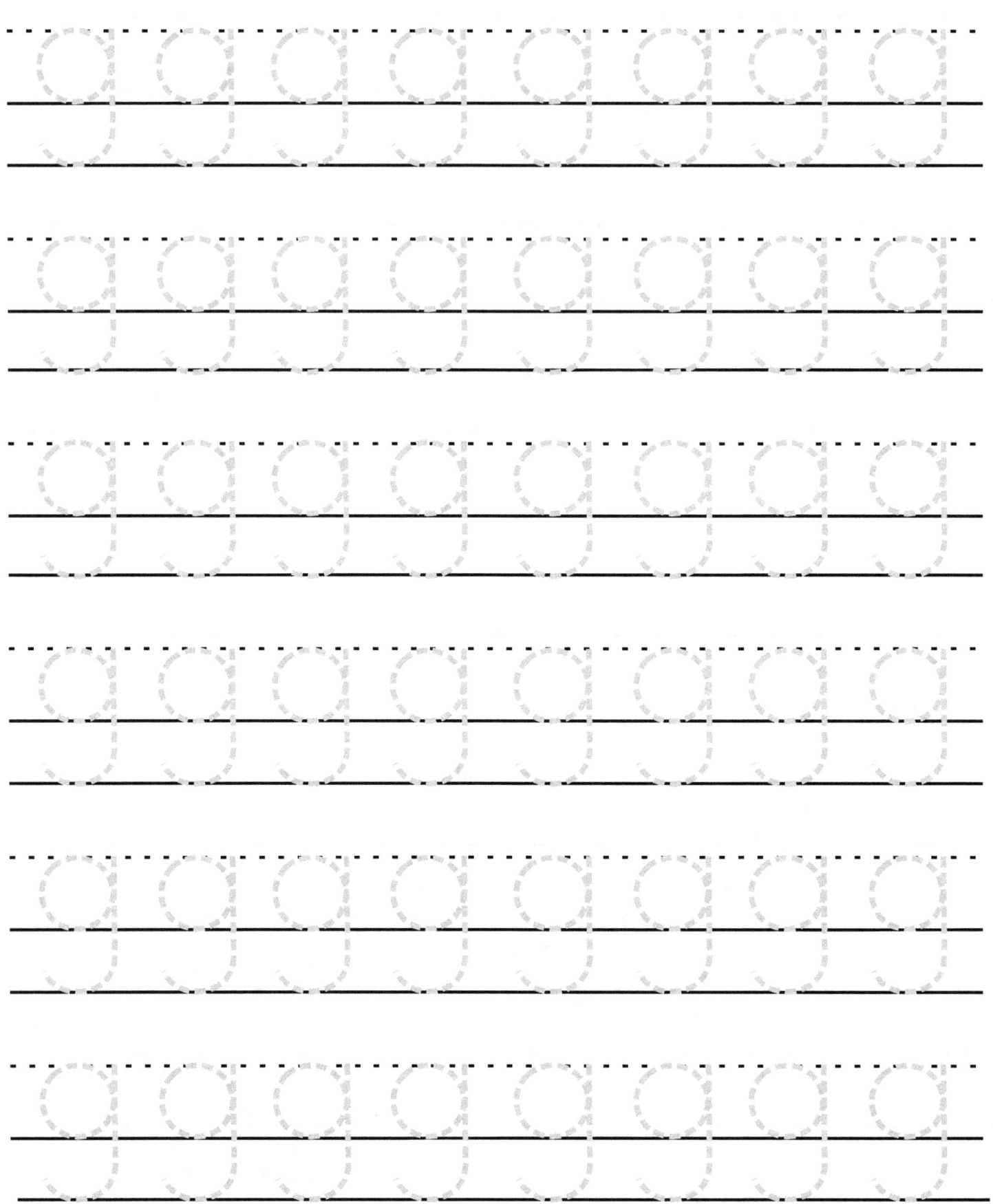

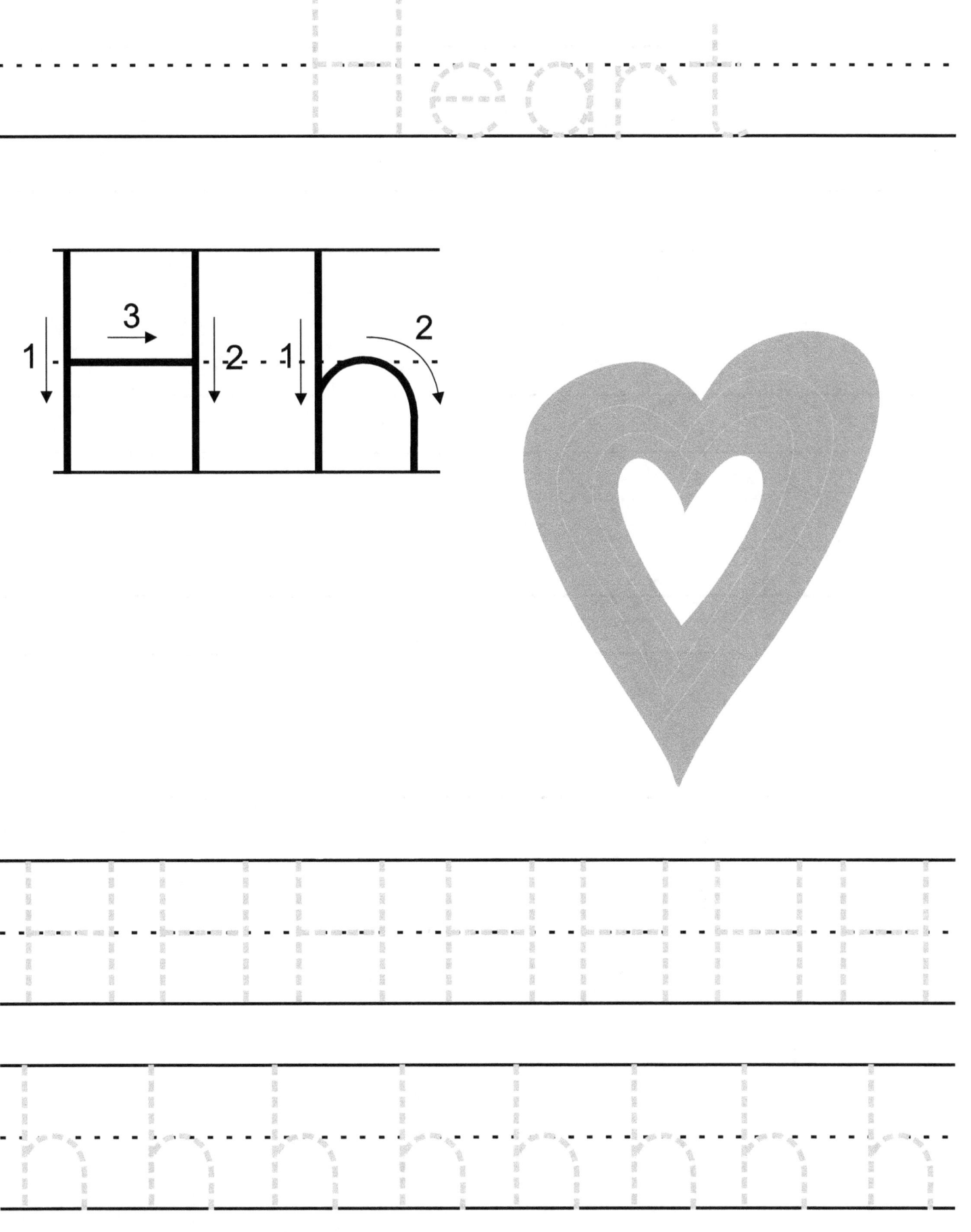

26

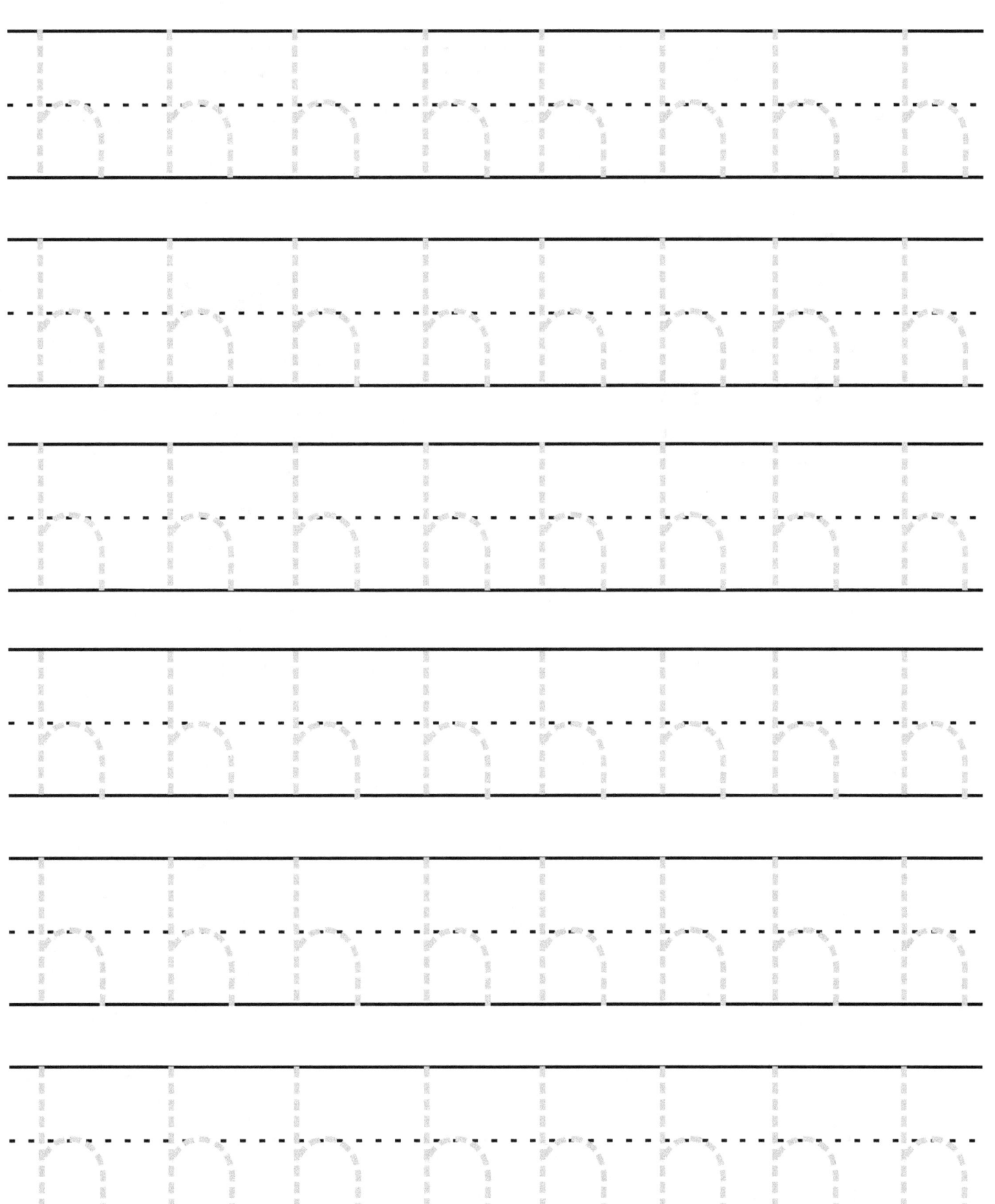

Ice cream

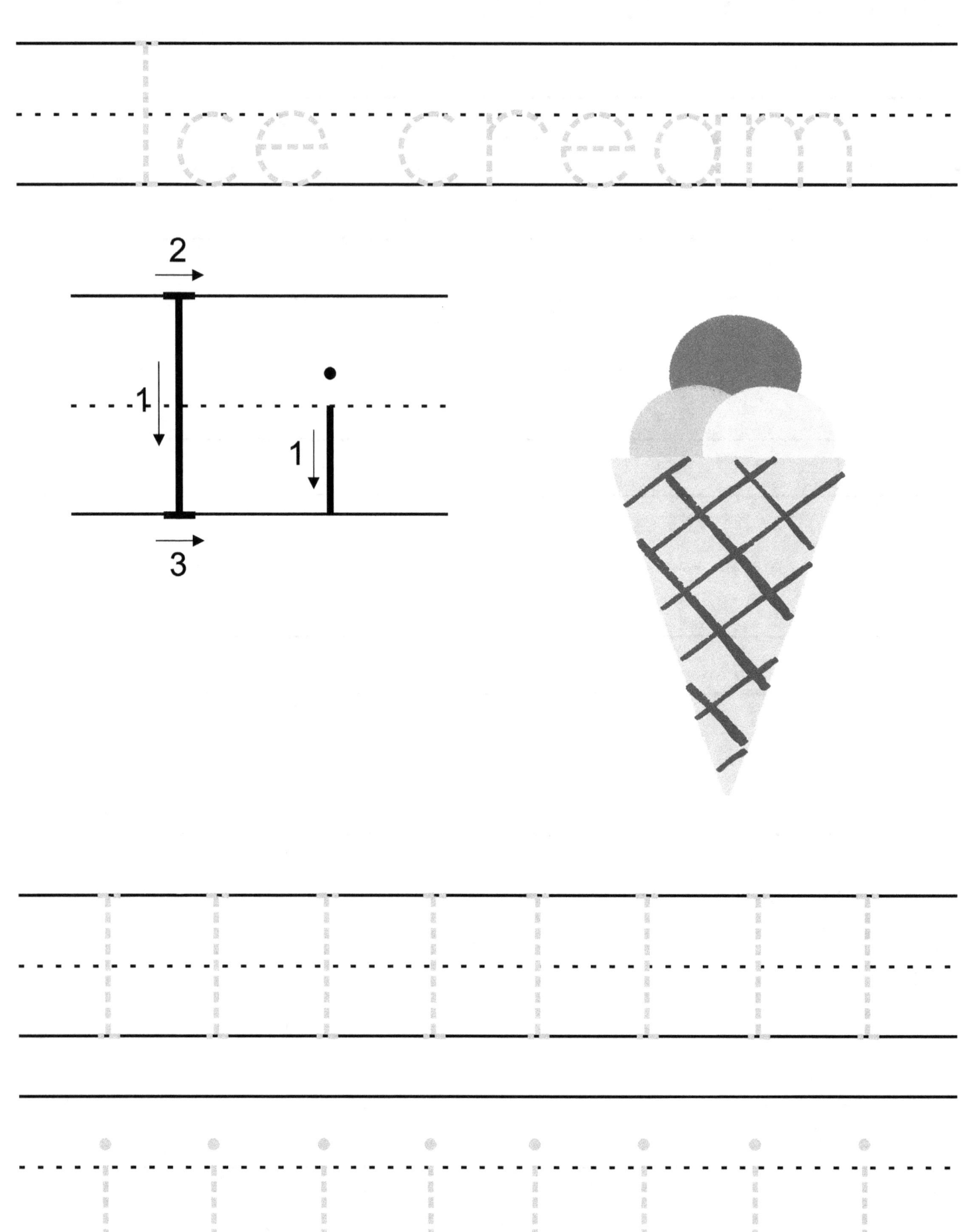

29

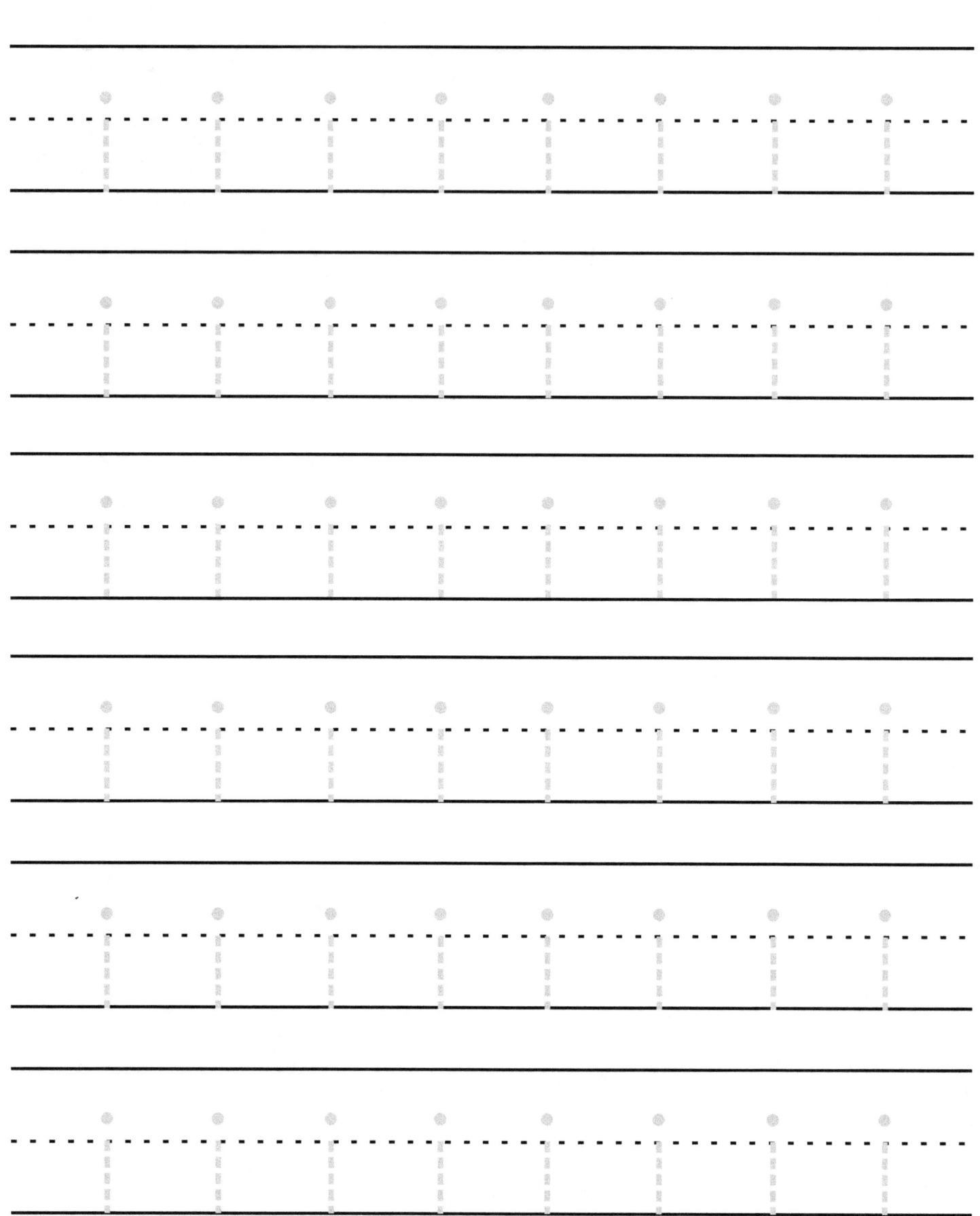

30

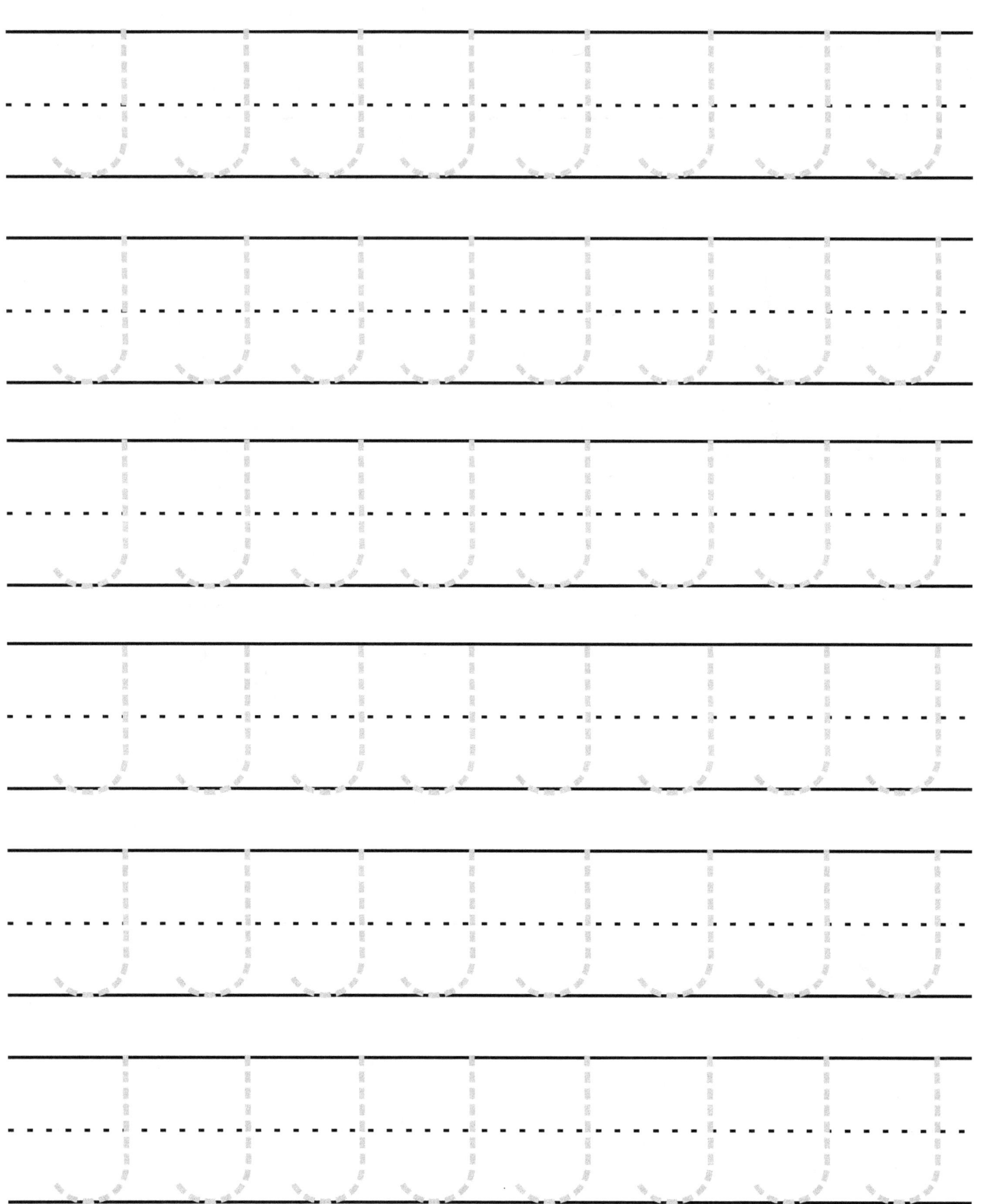

33

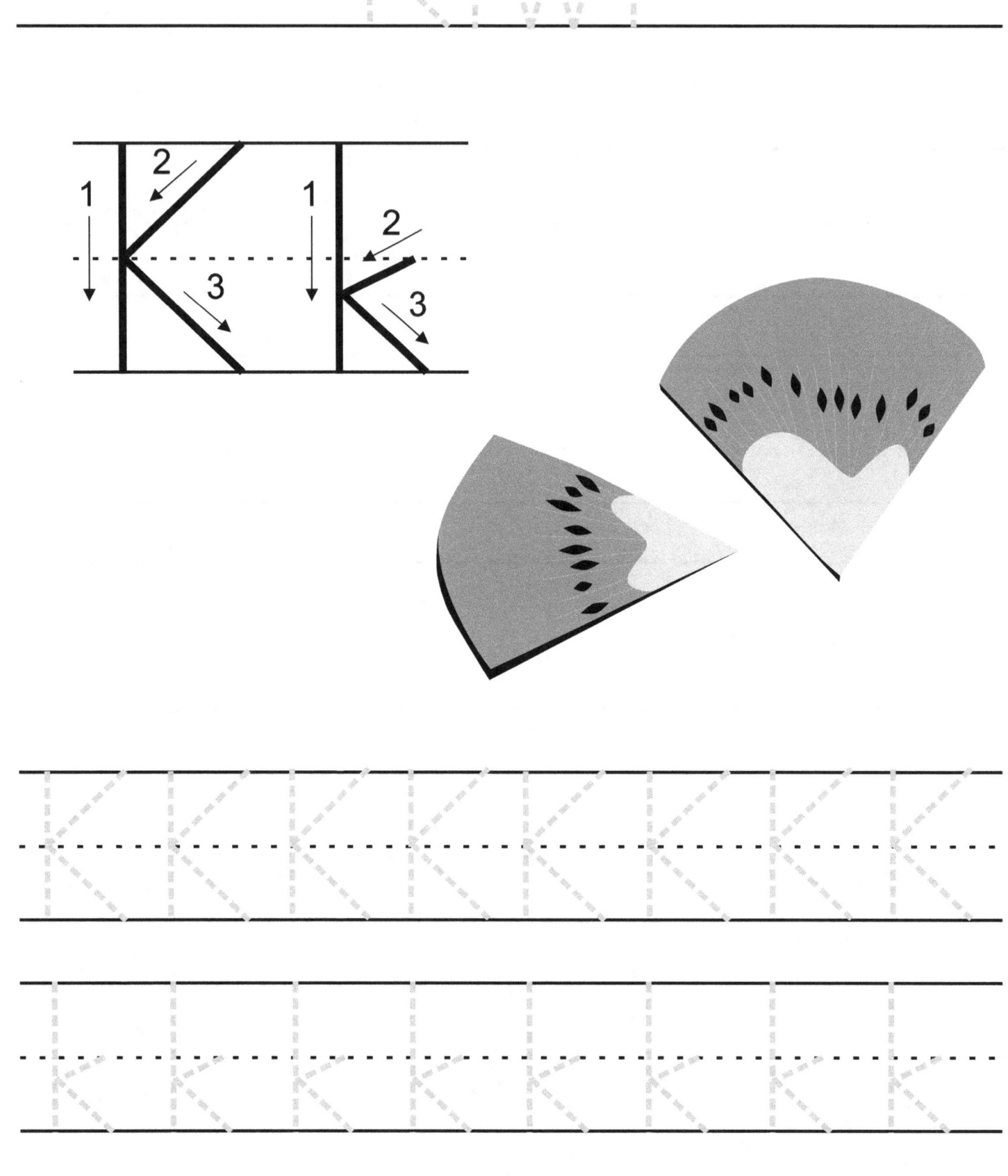

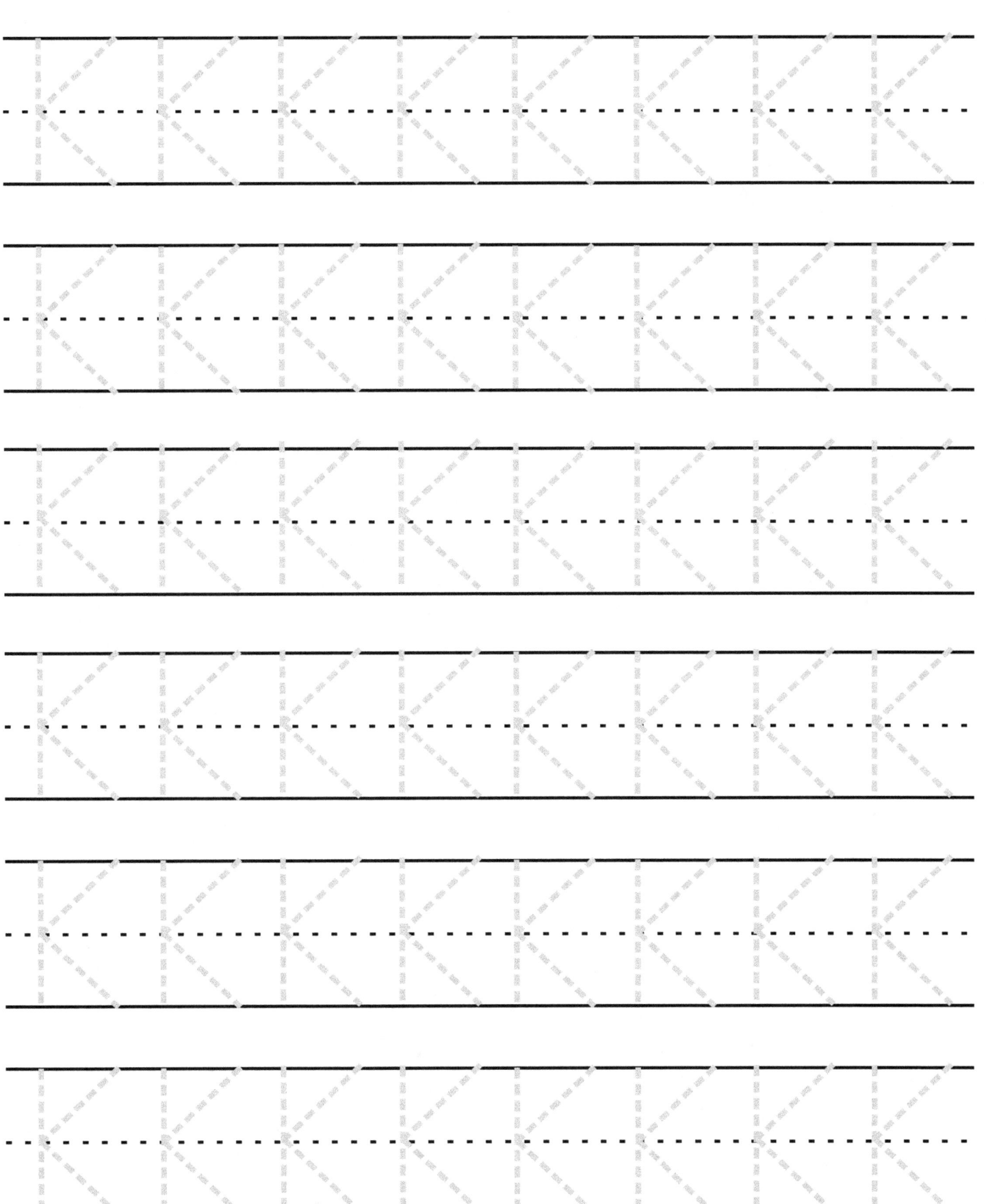

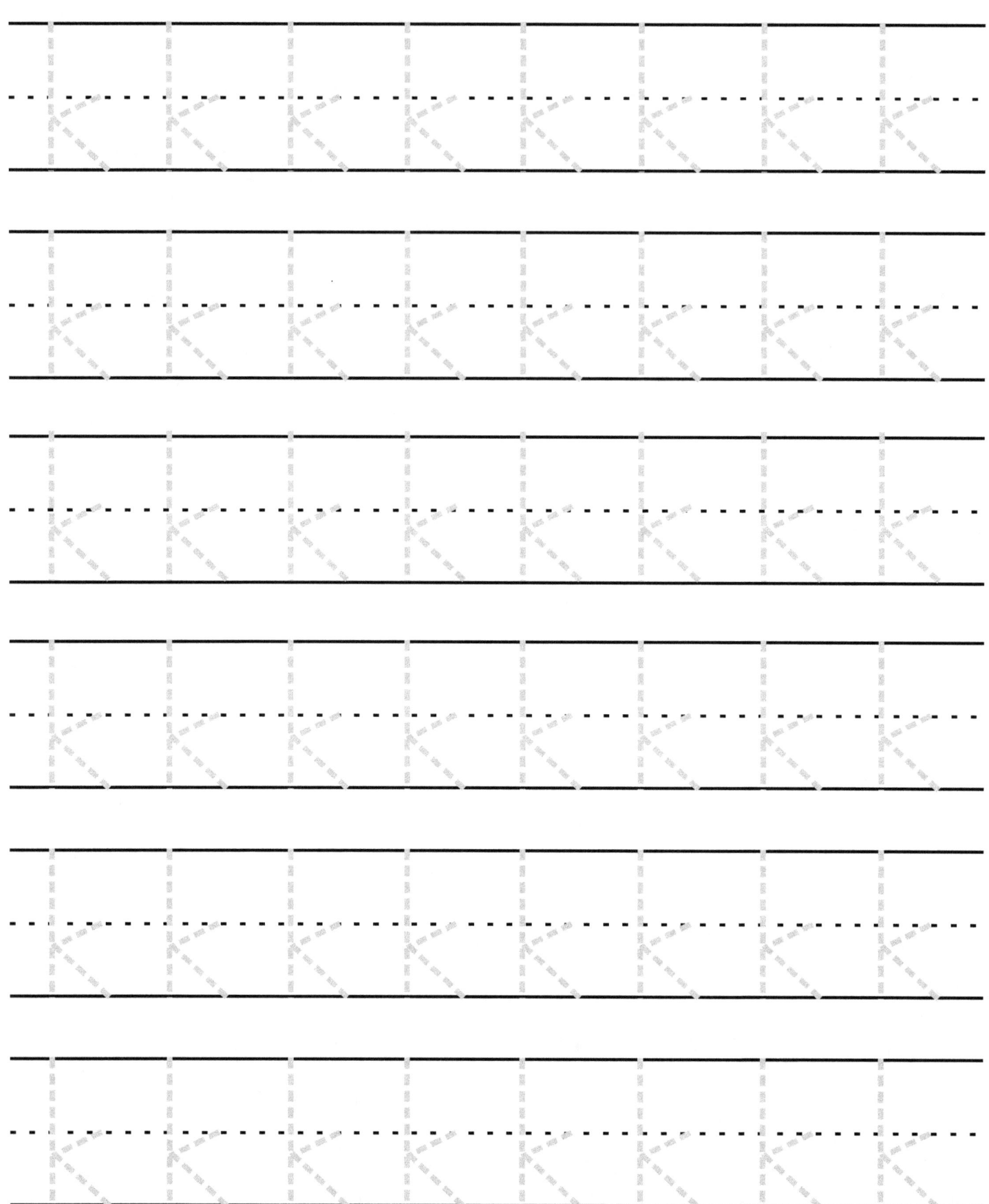

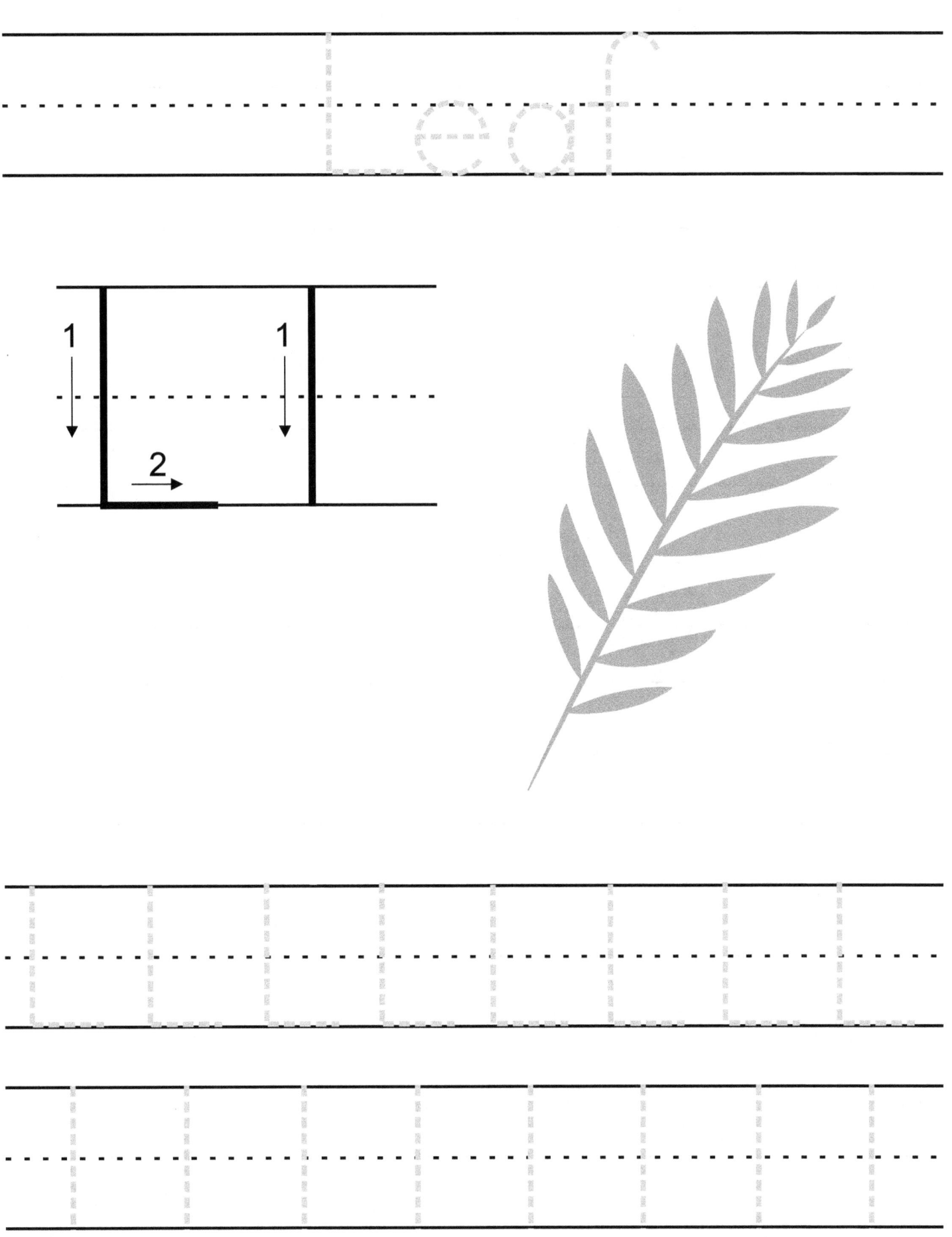

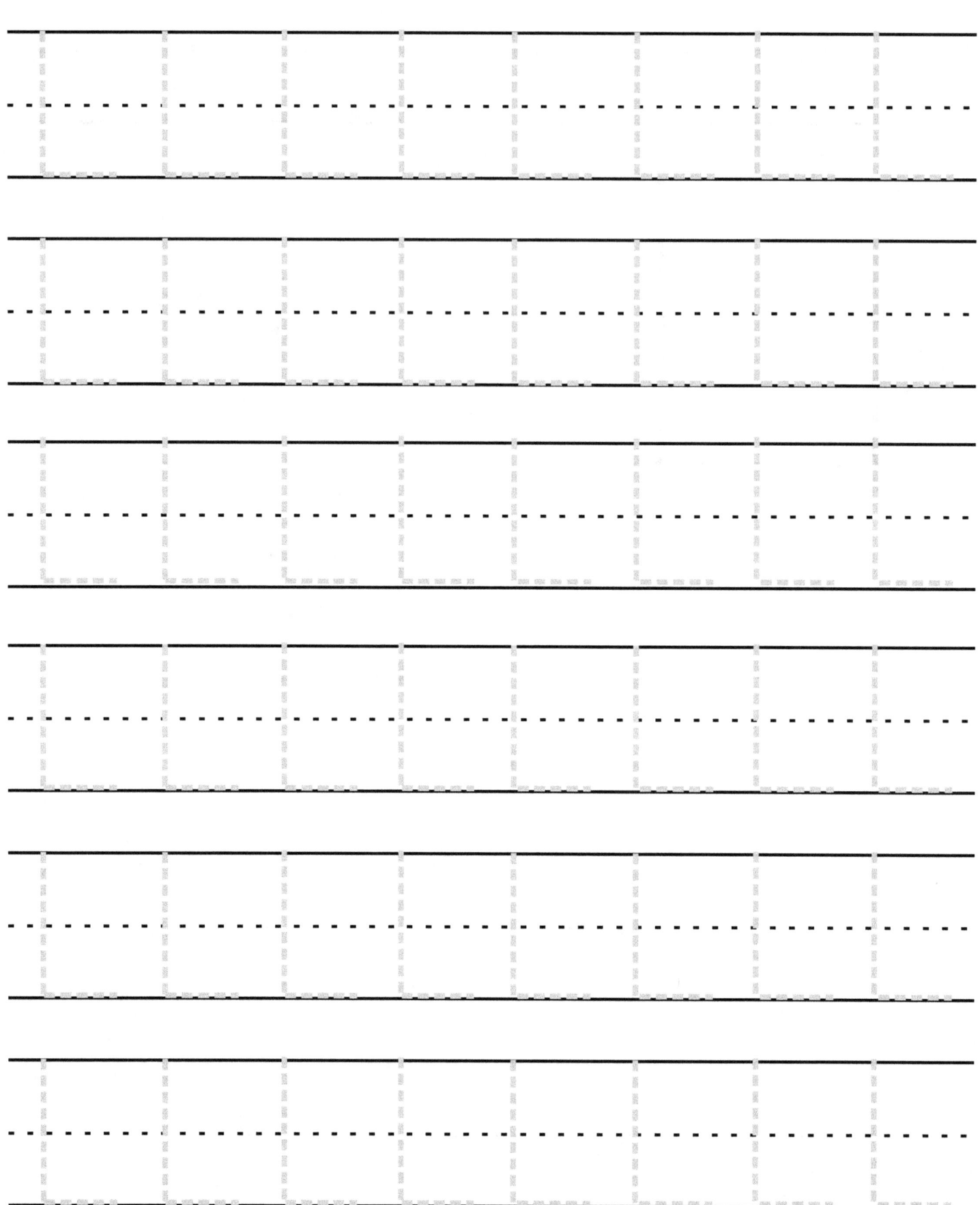

39

Money

Mm

MMMM

mmmmm

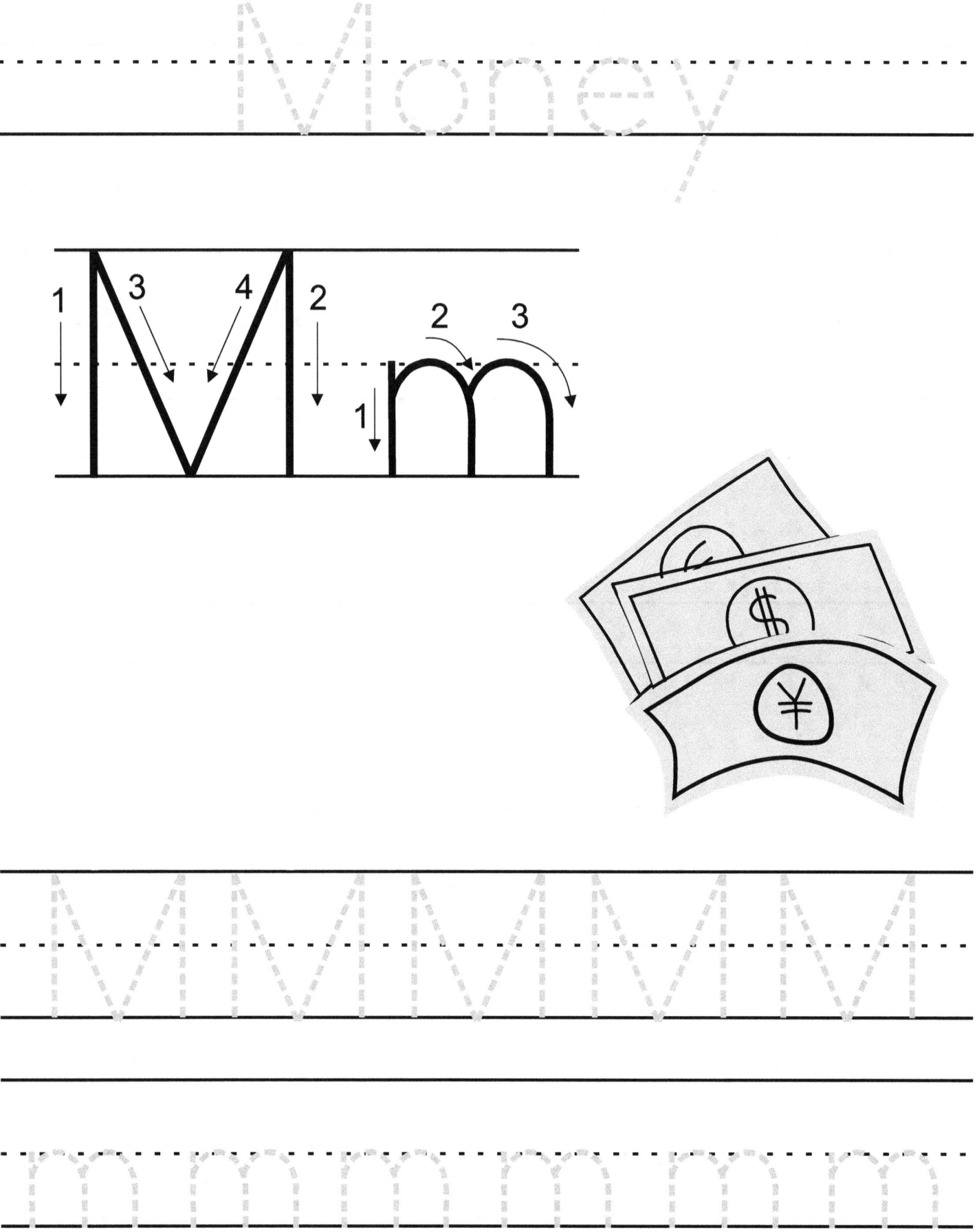

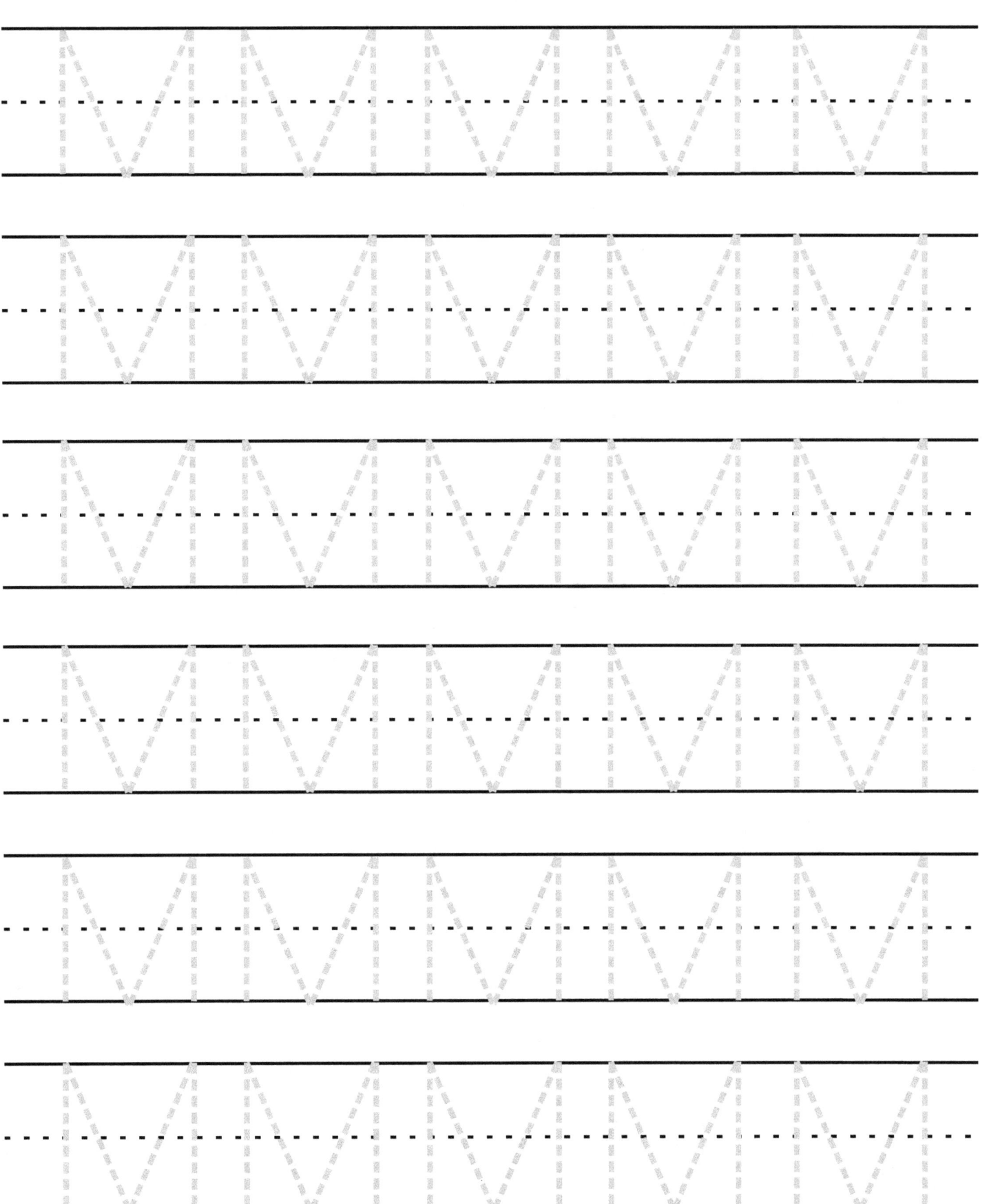

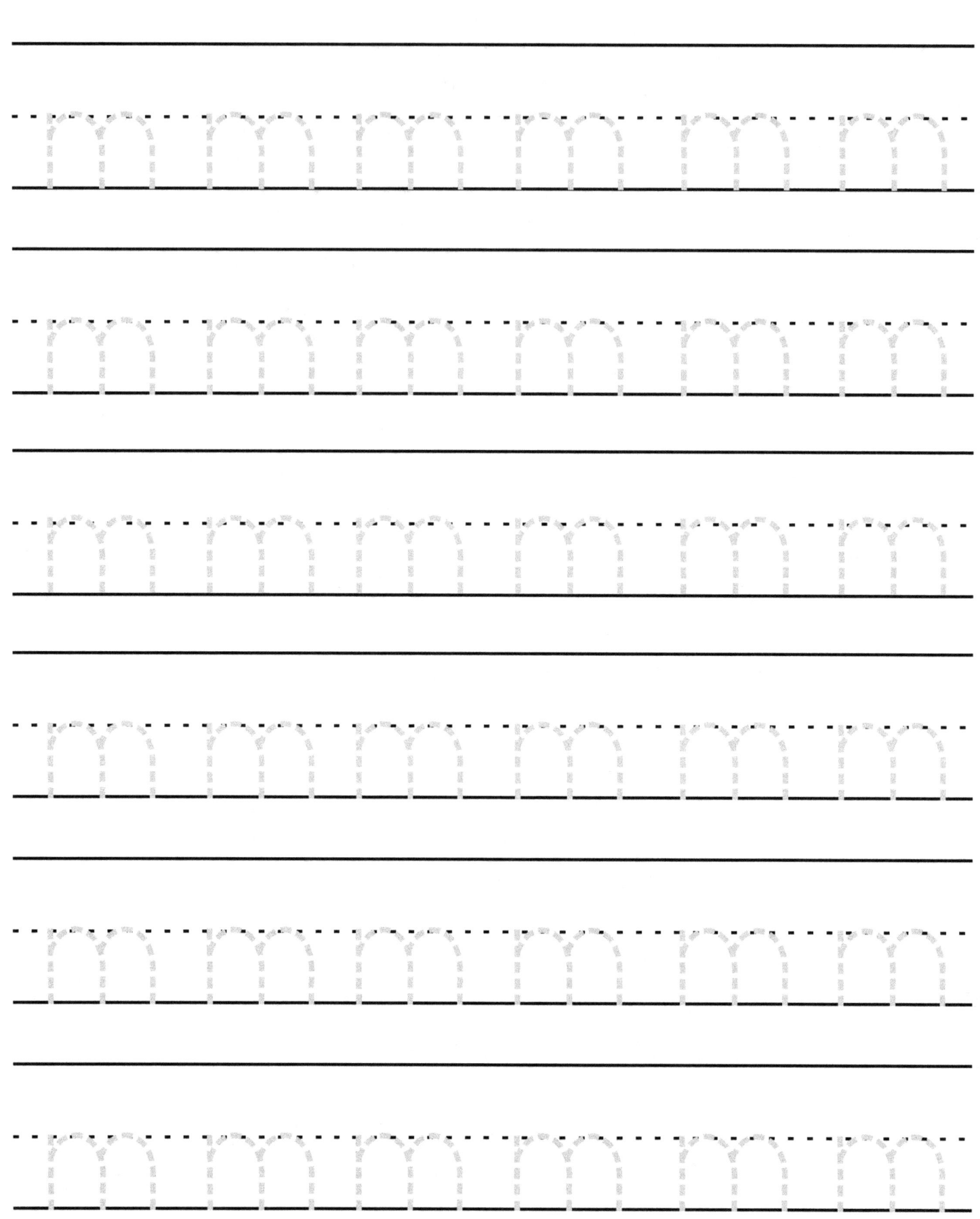

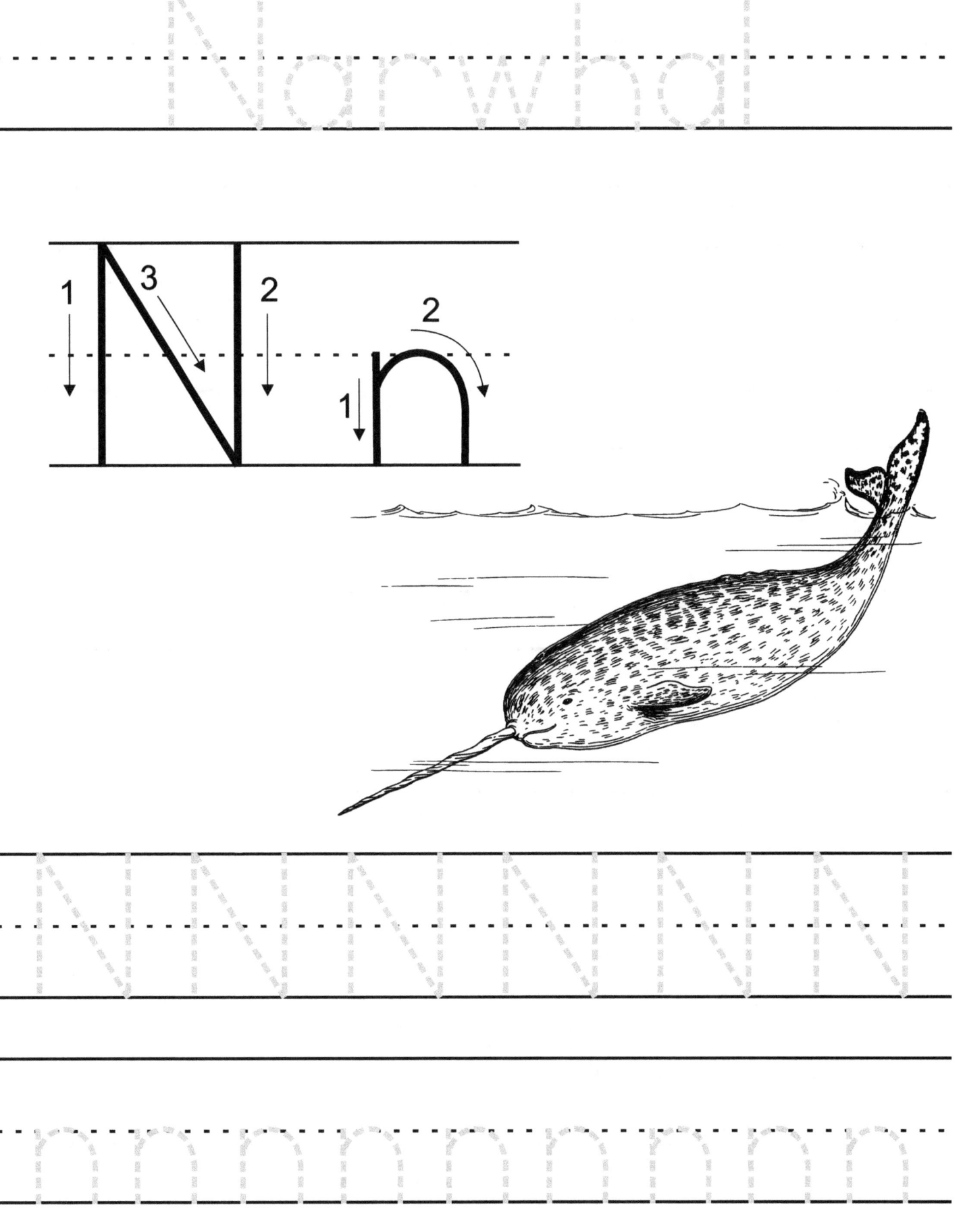

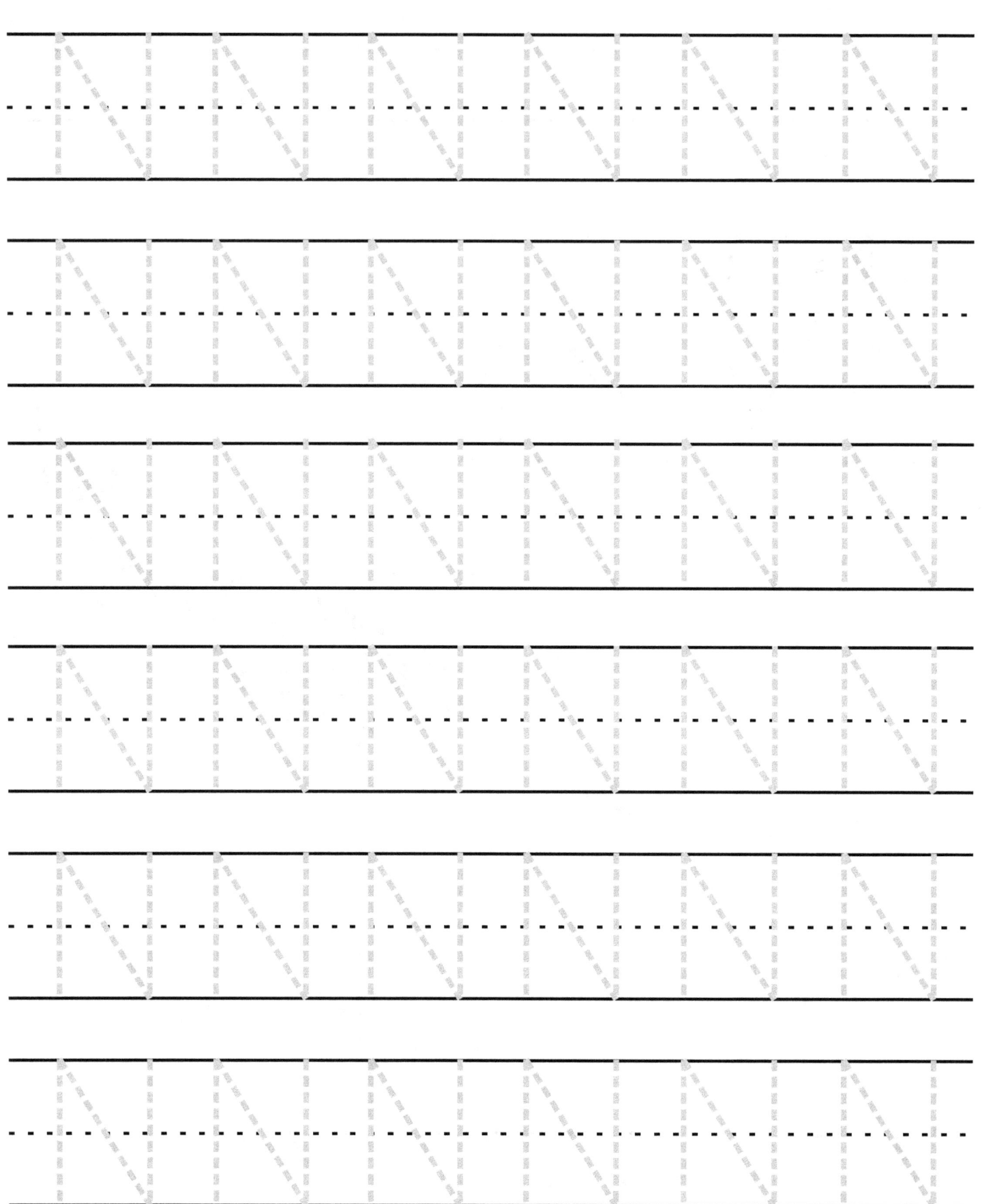

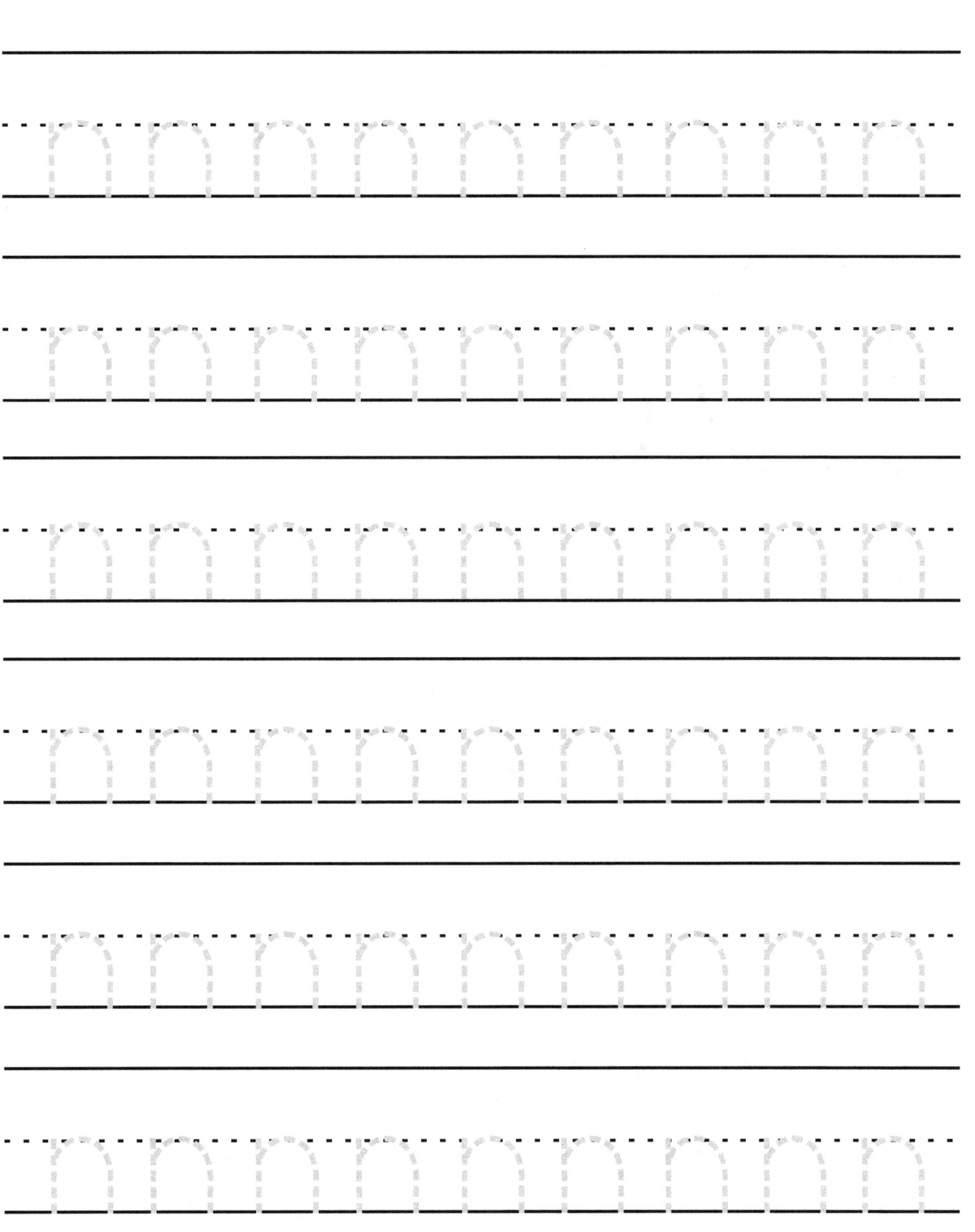

Owl

47

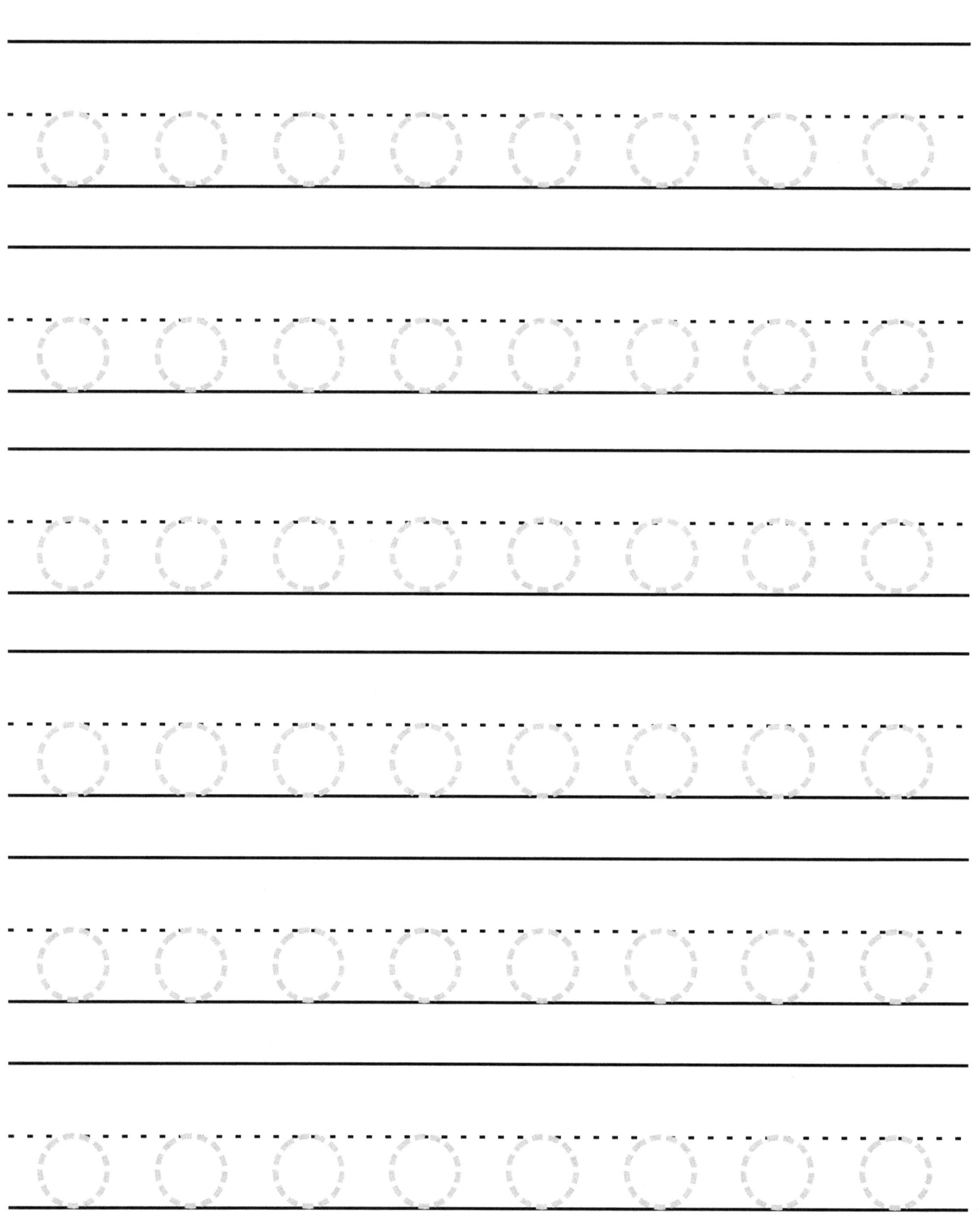

Police

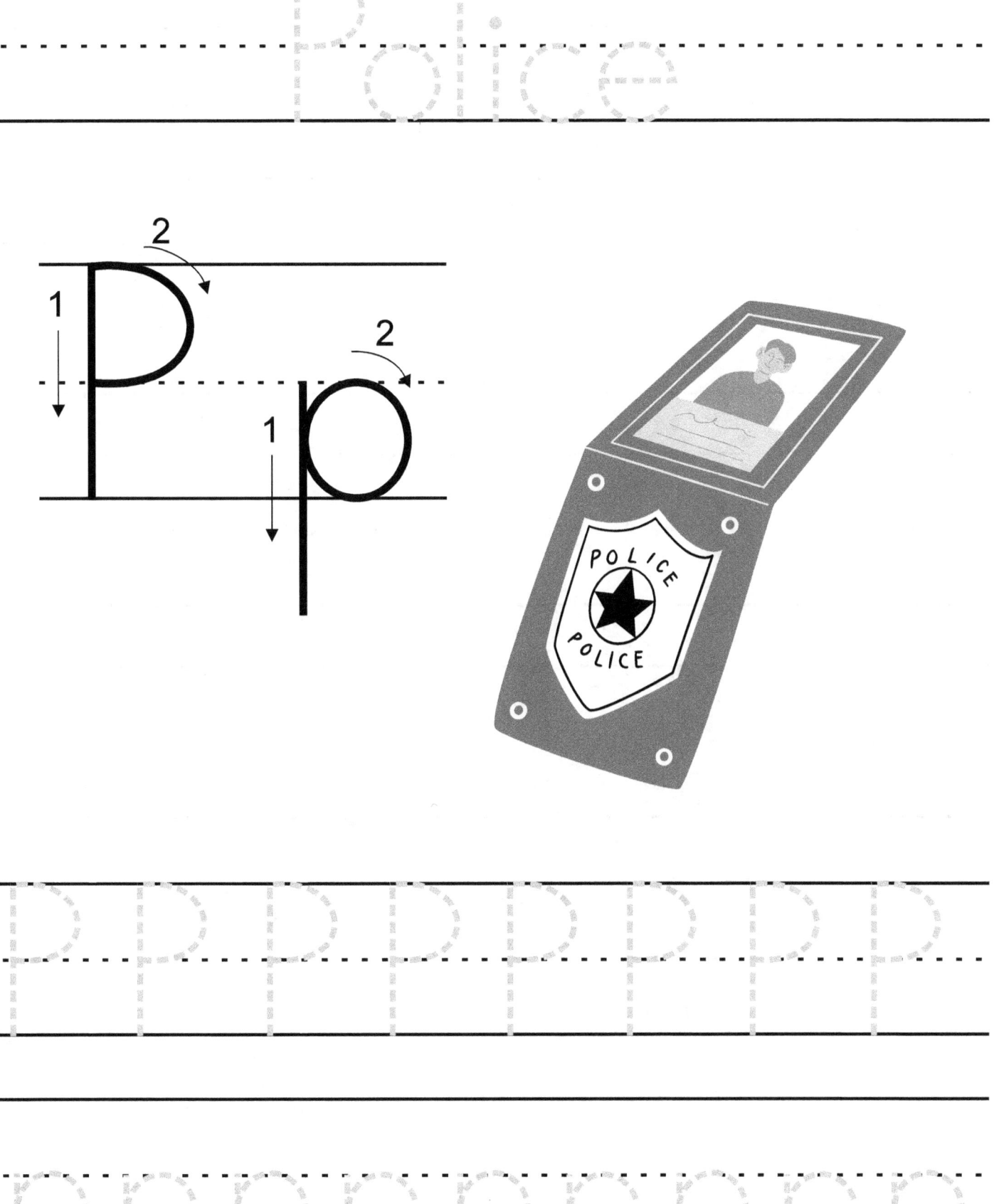

50

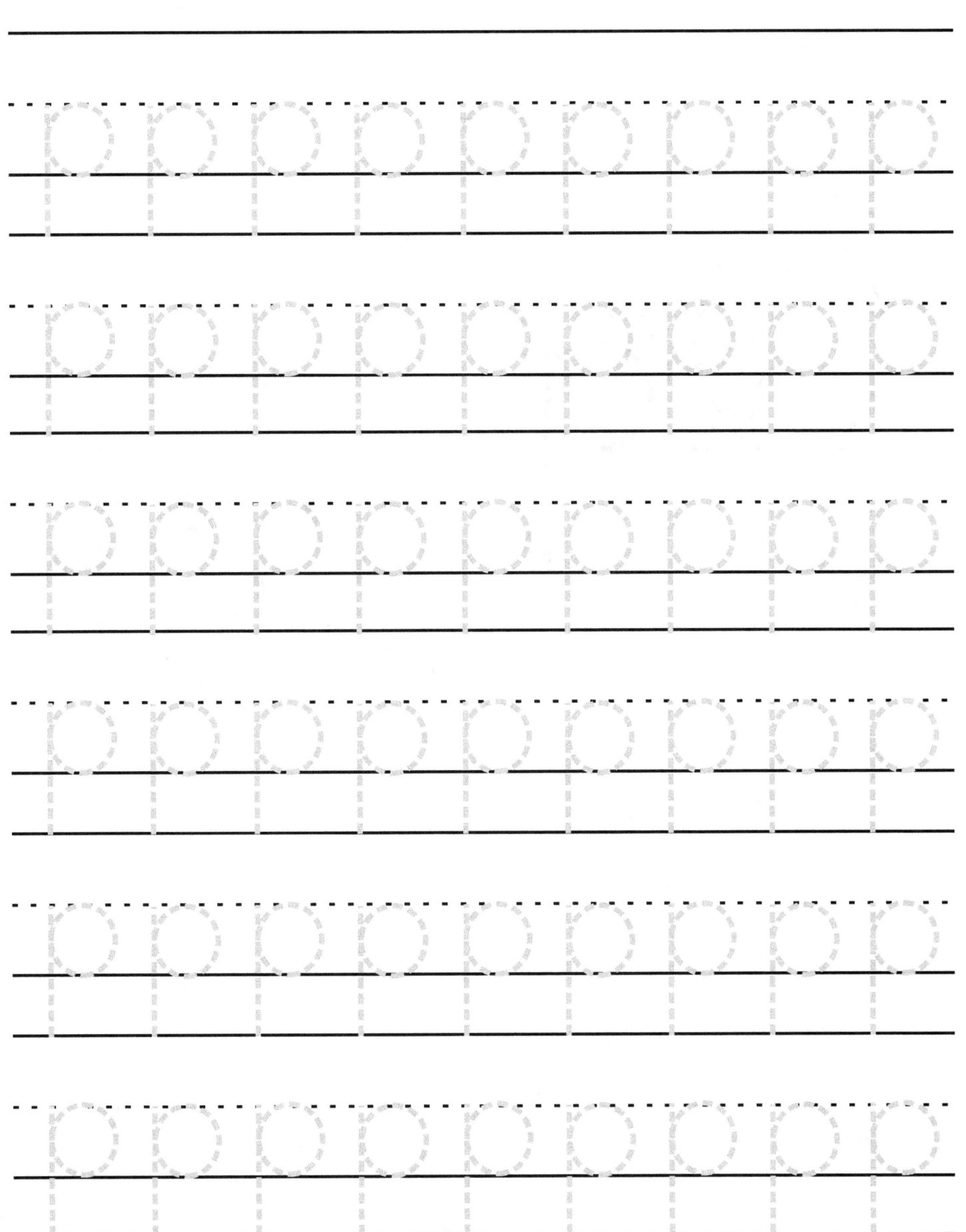

Quadrant

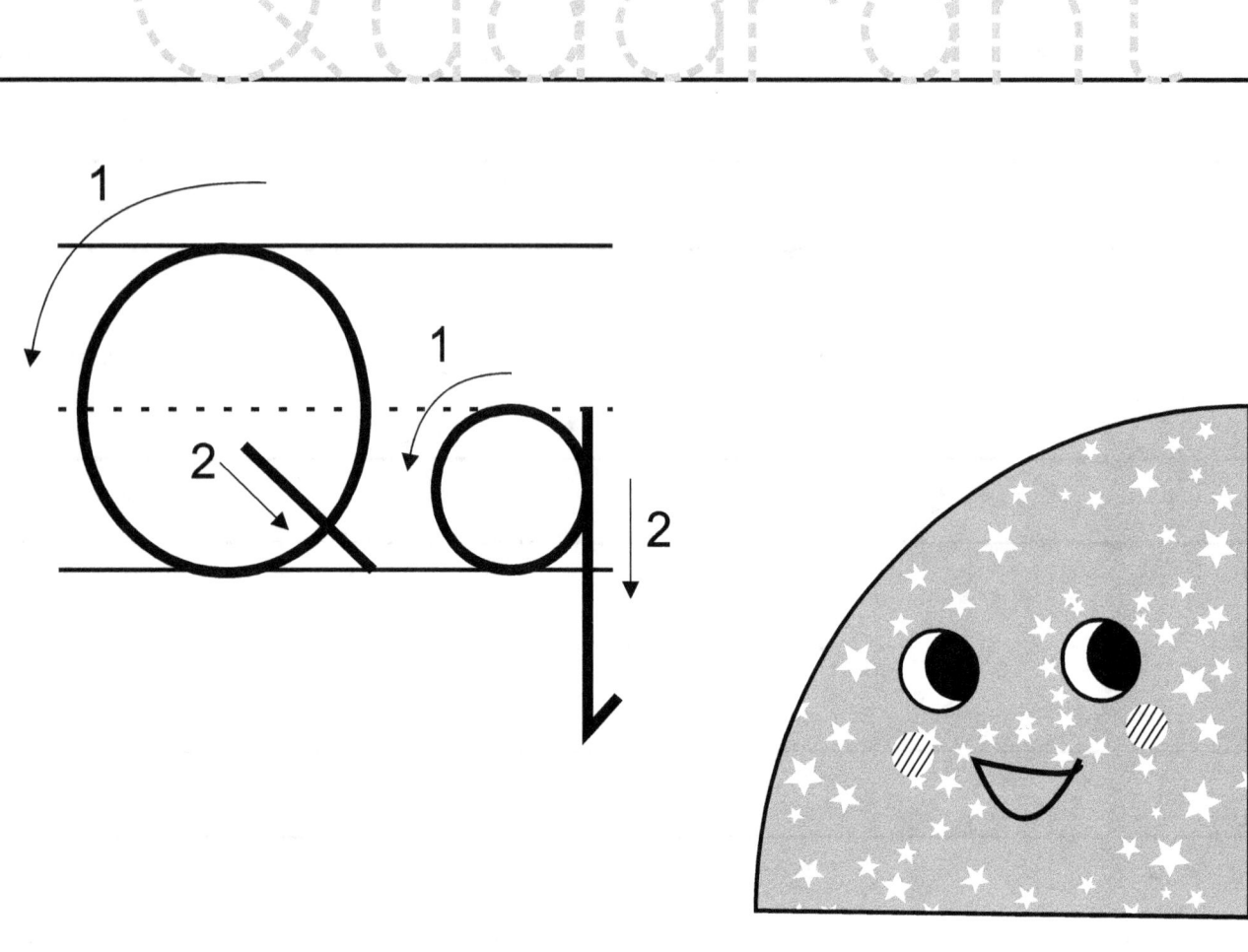

Q q Q q Q

q q q q q q q

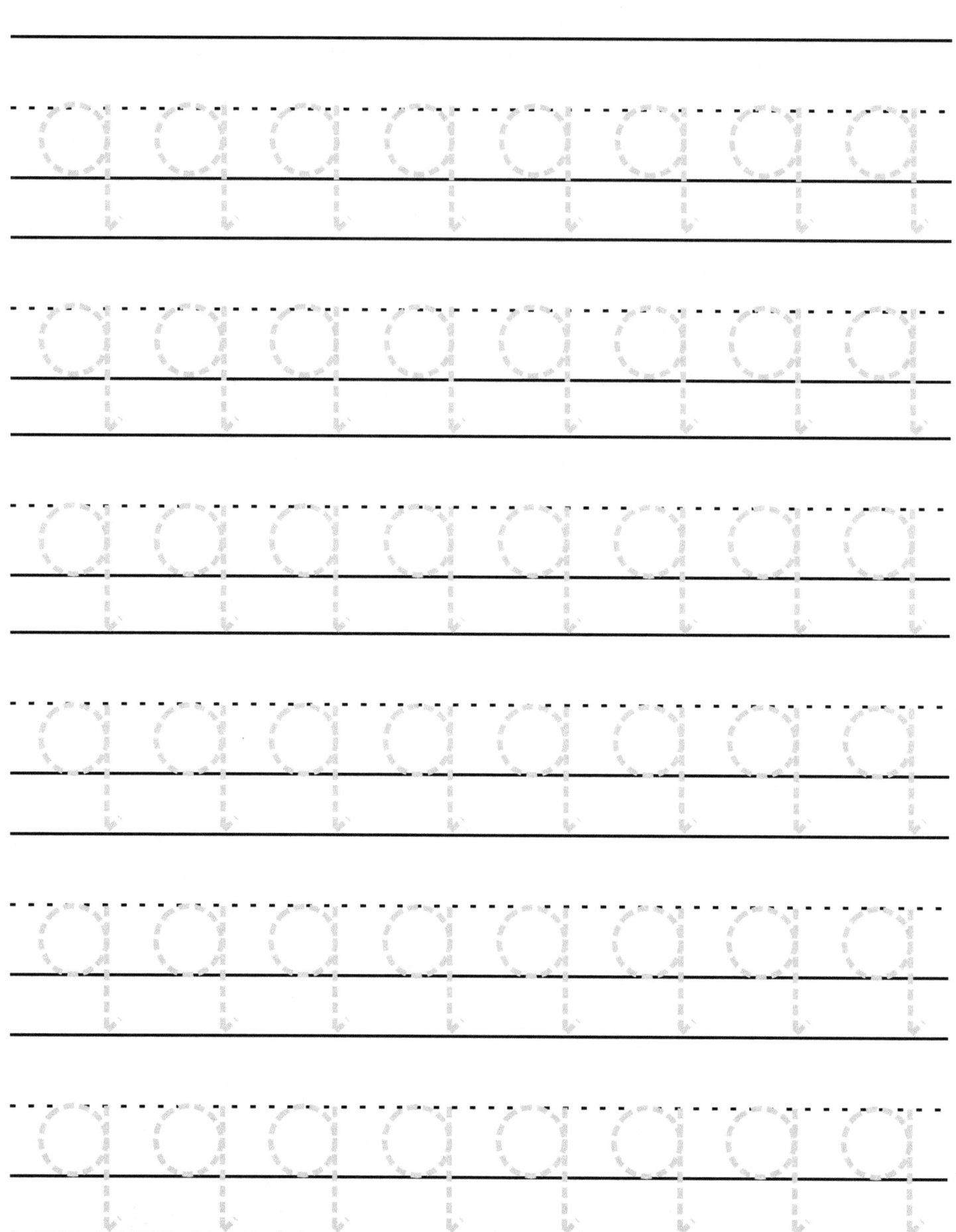

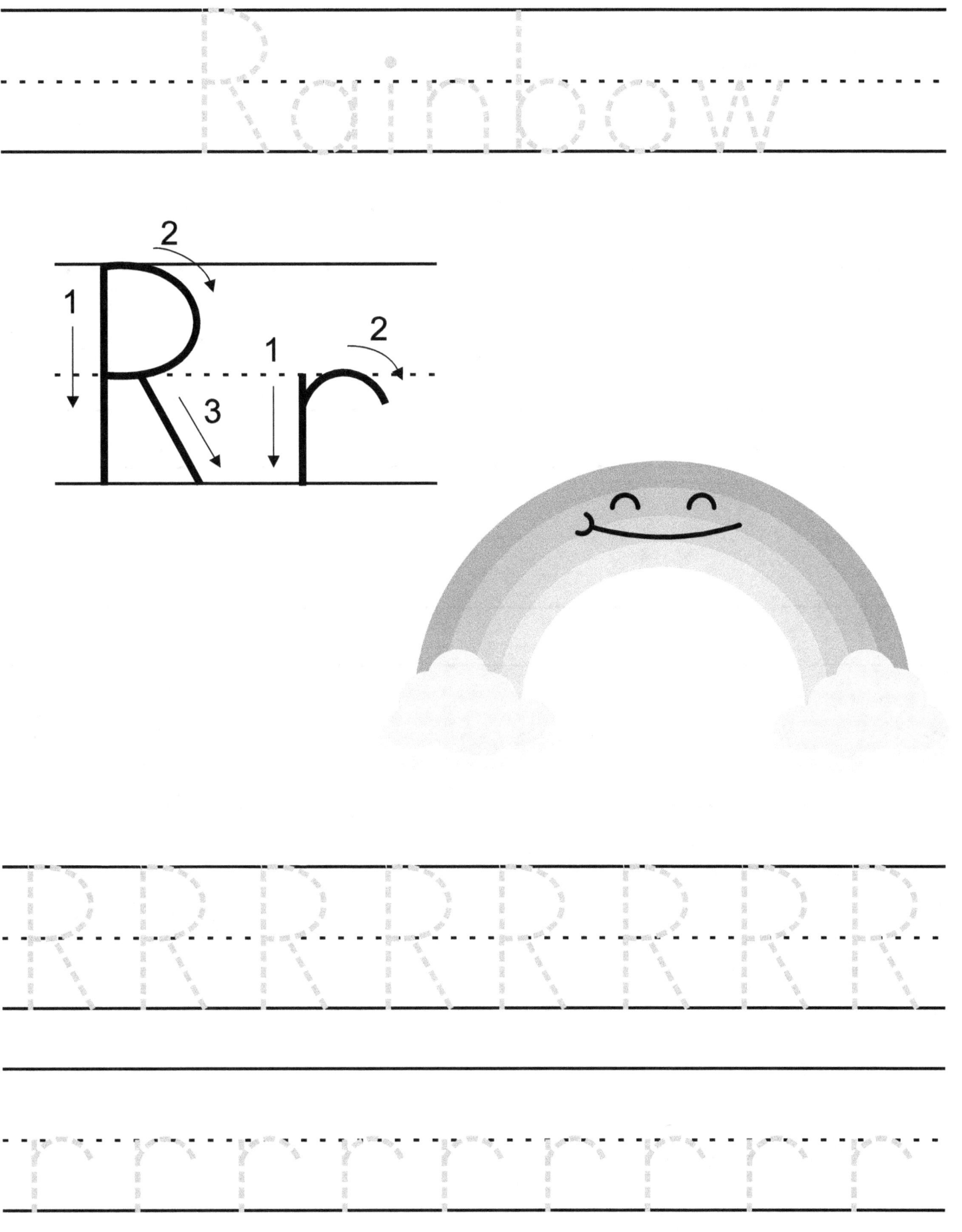

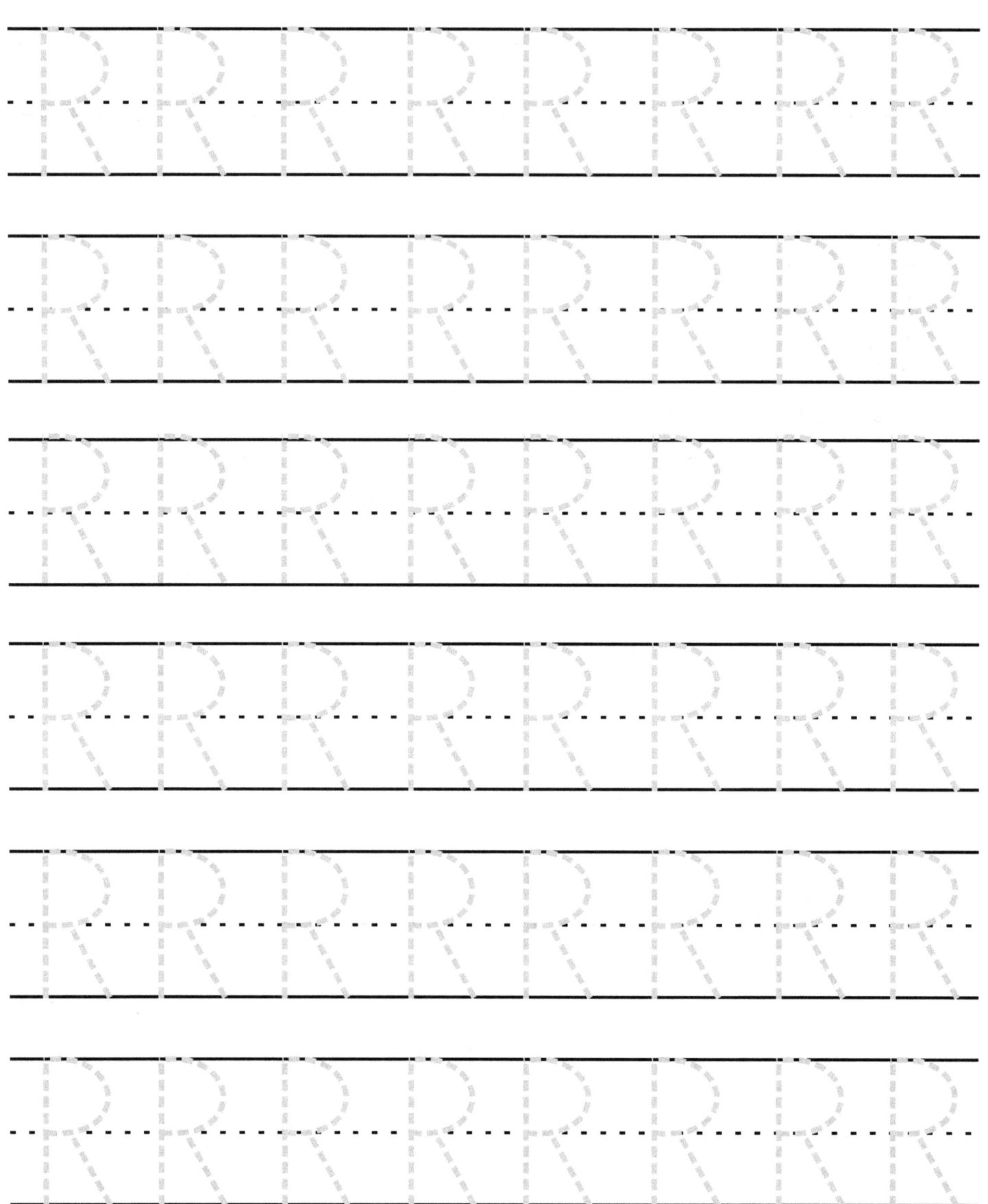

56

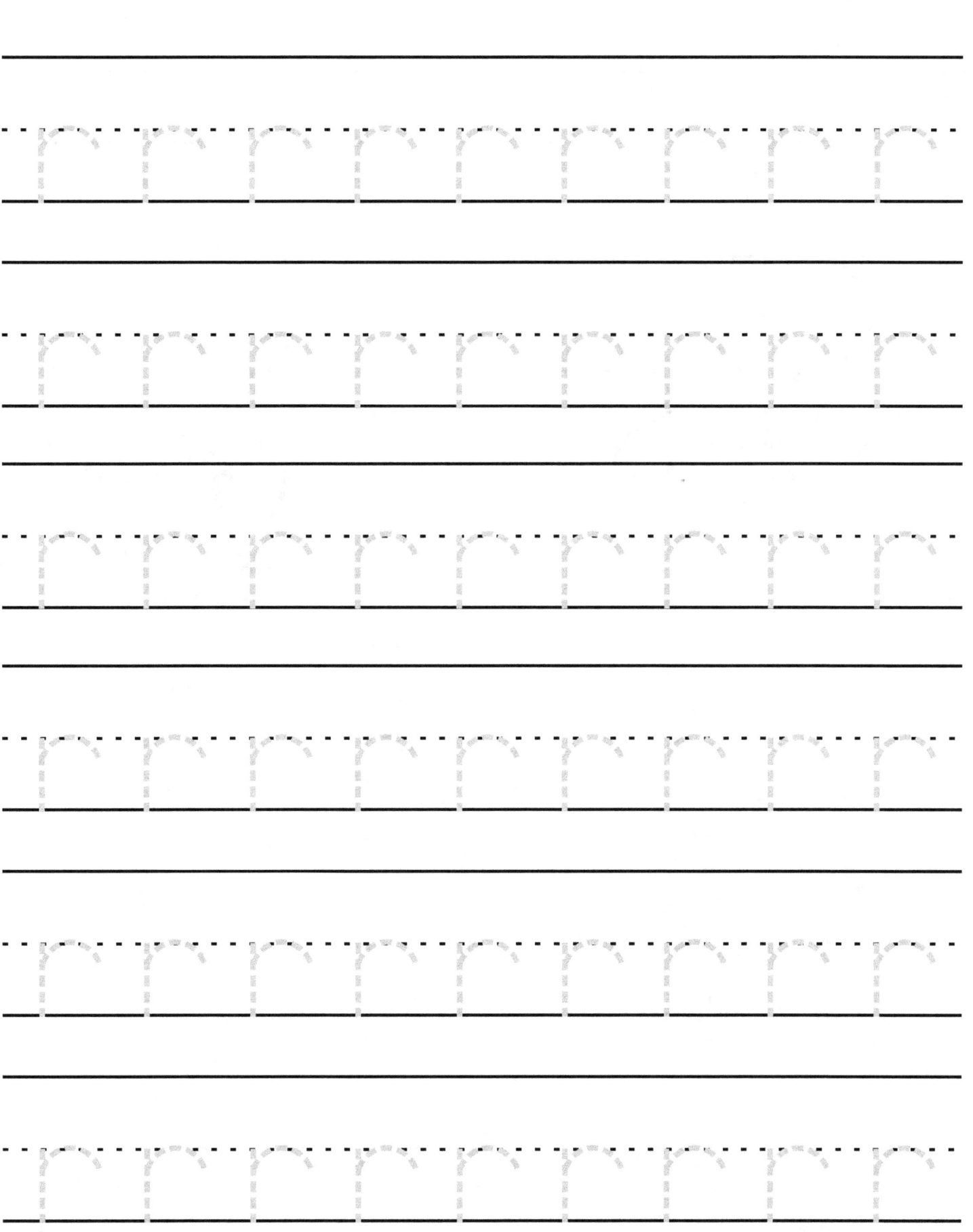

sssssss

sssssss

sssssss

sssssss

sssssss

sssssss

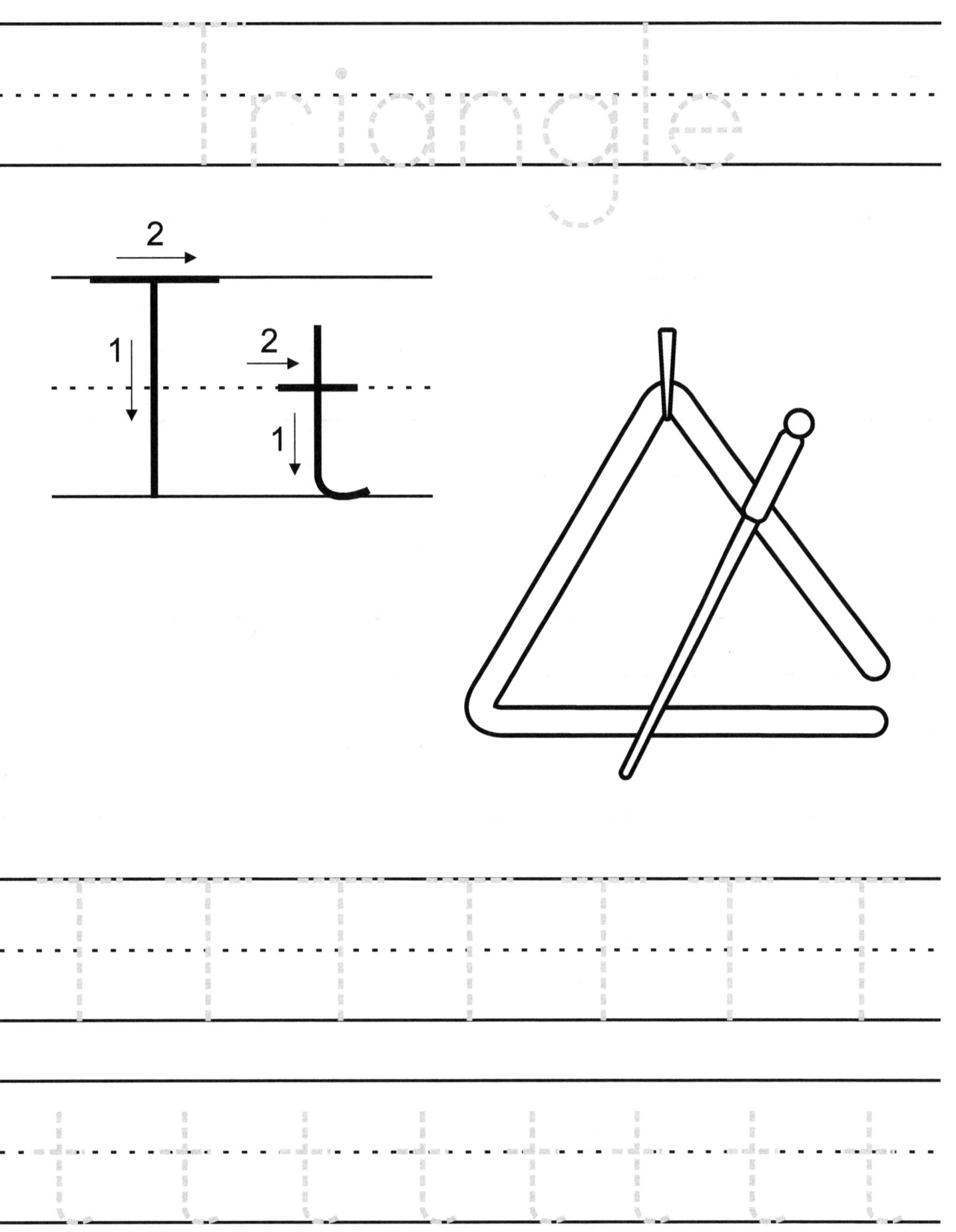

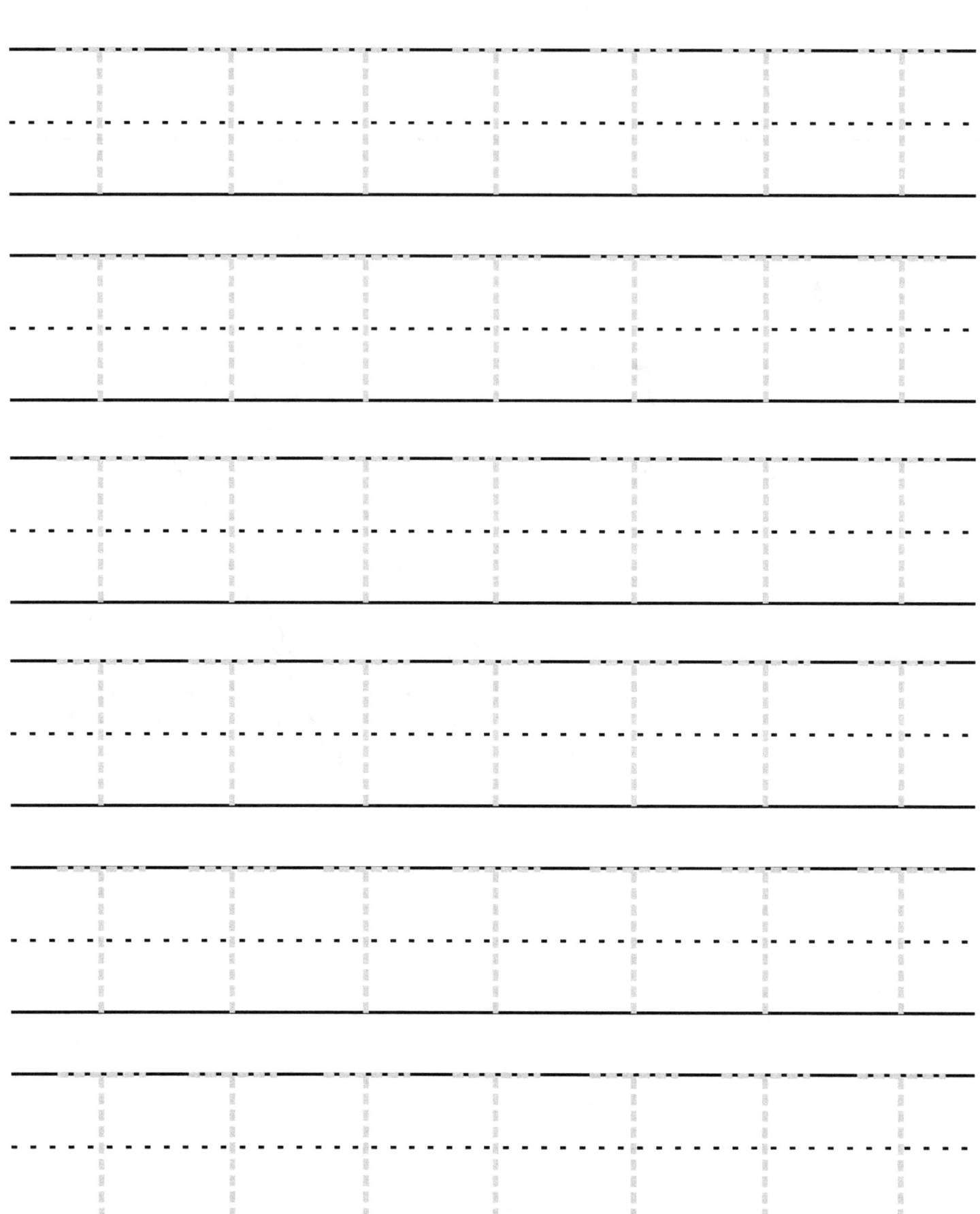

63

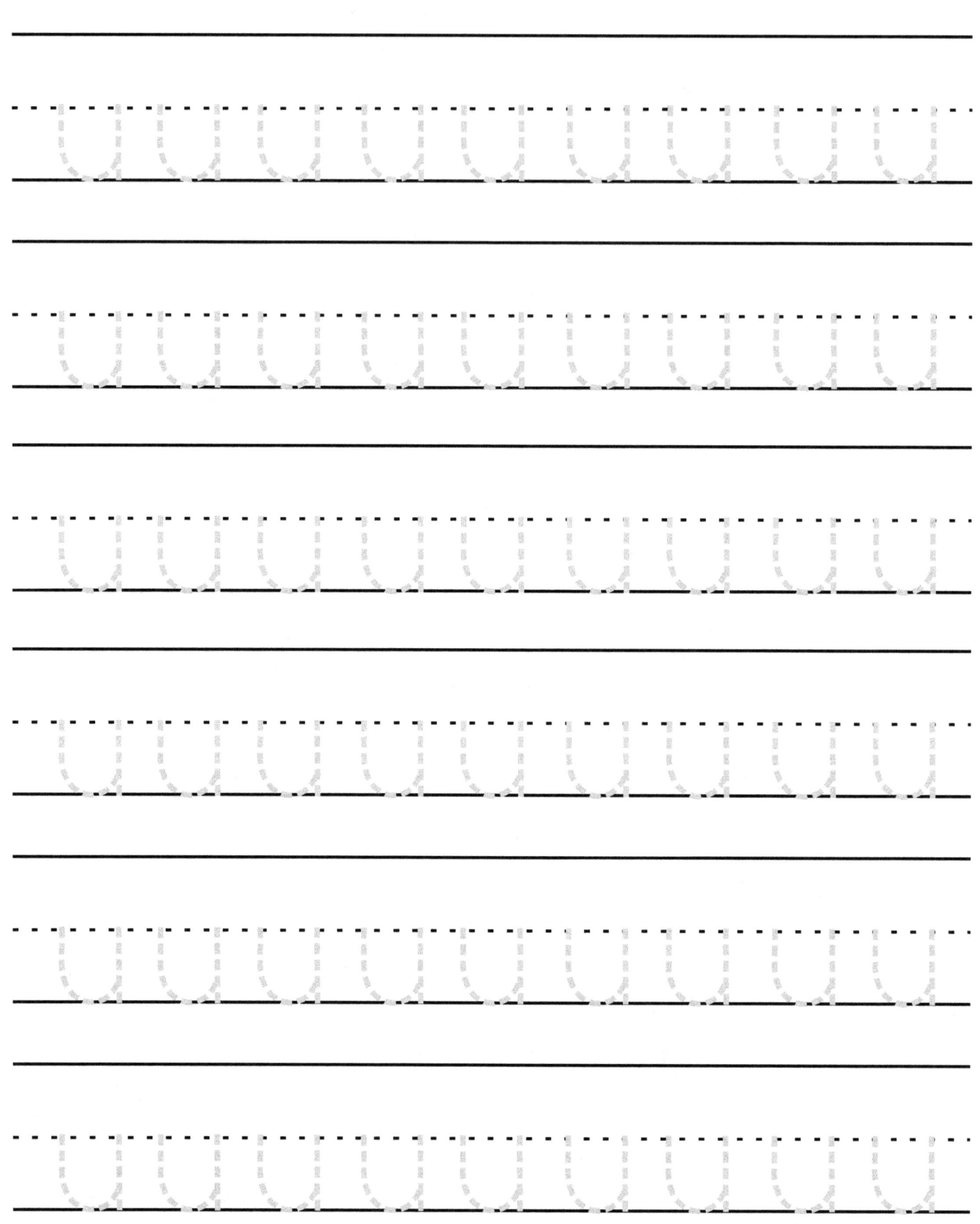

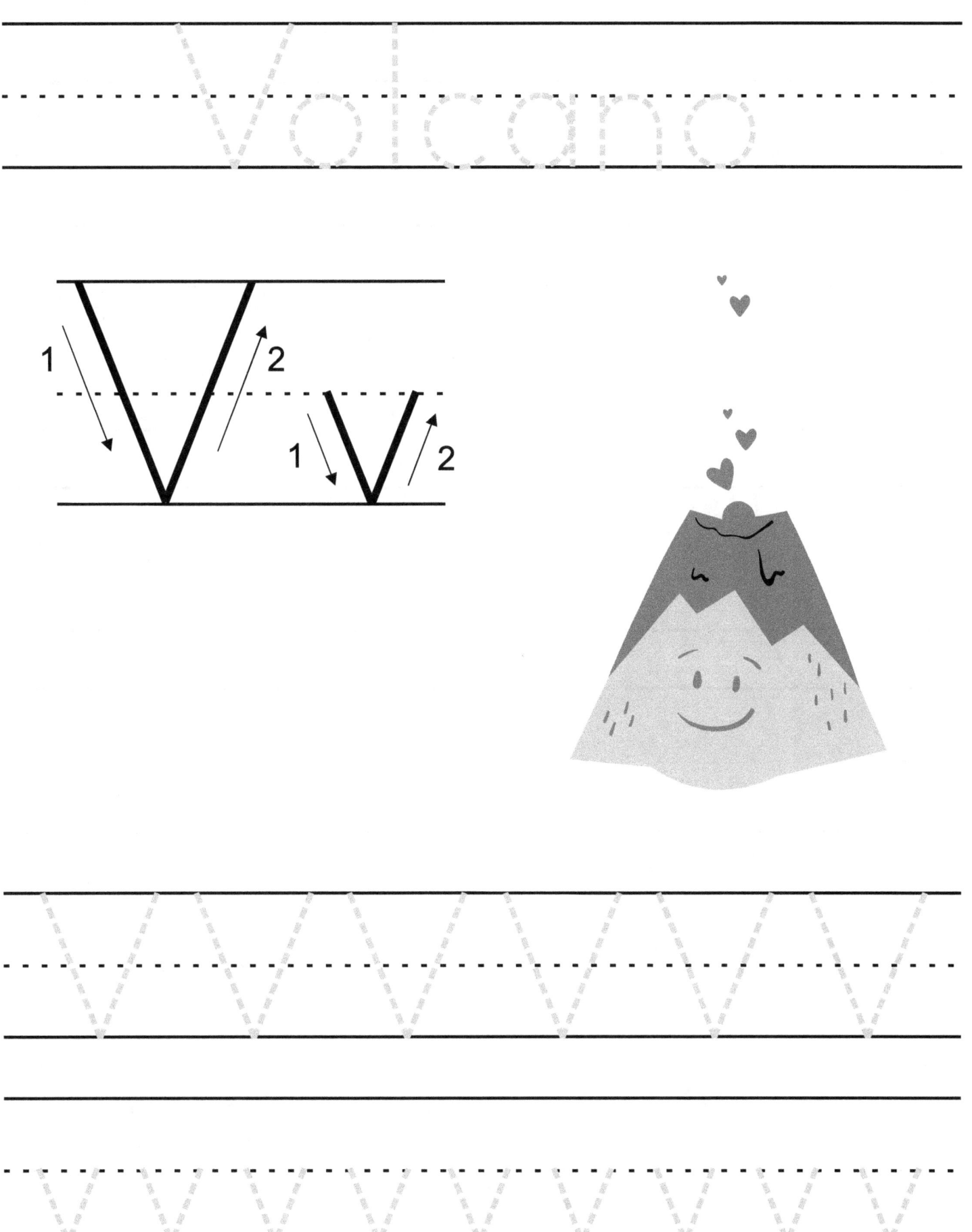

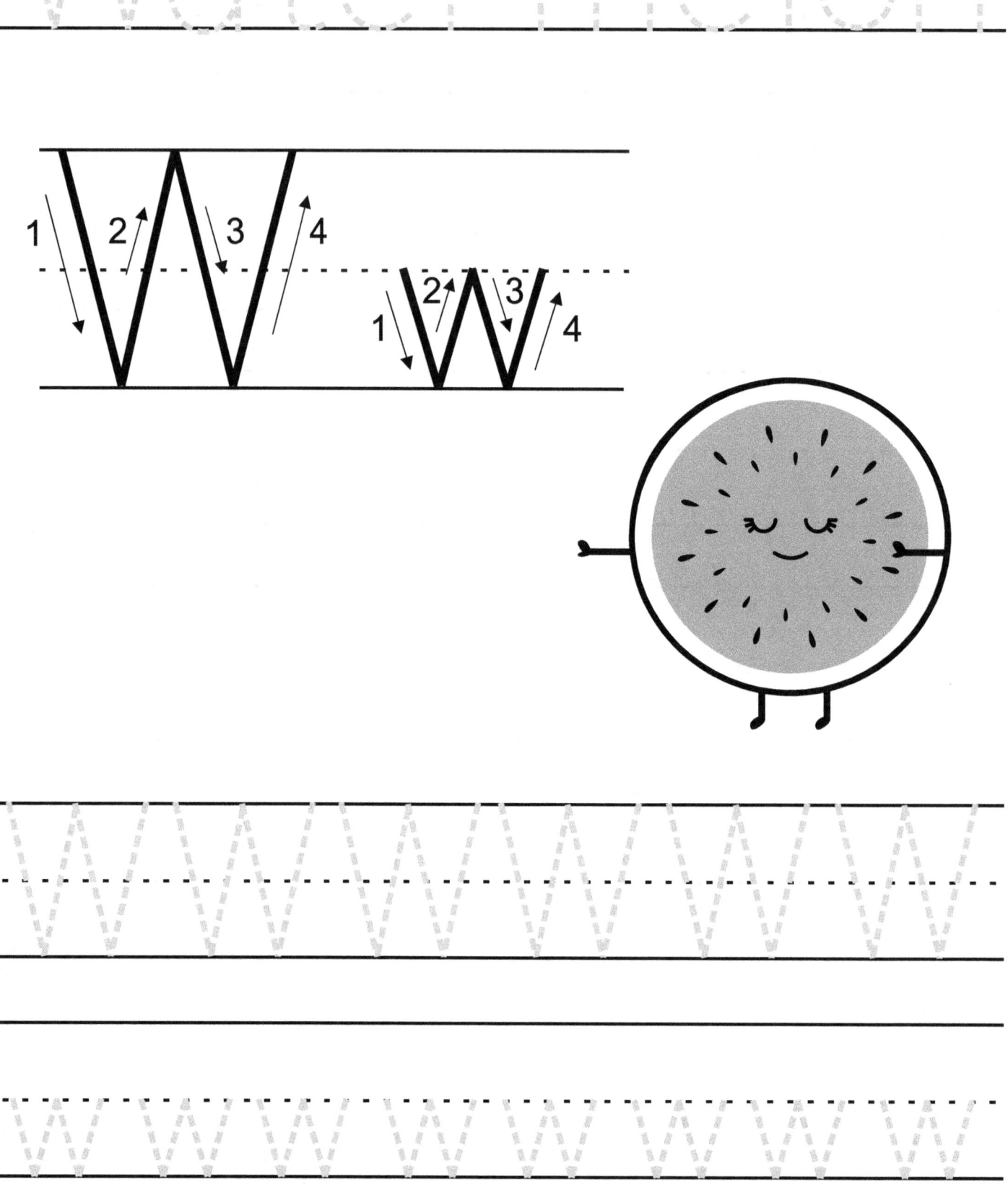

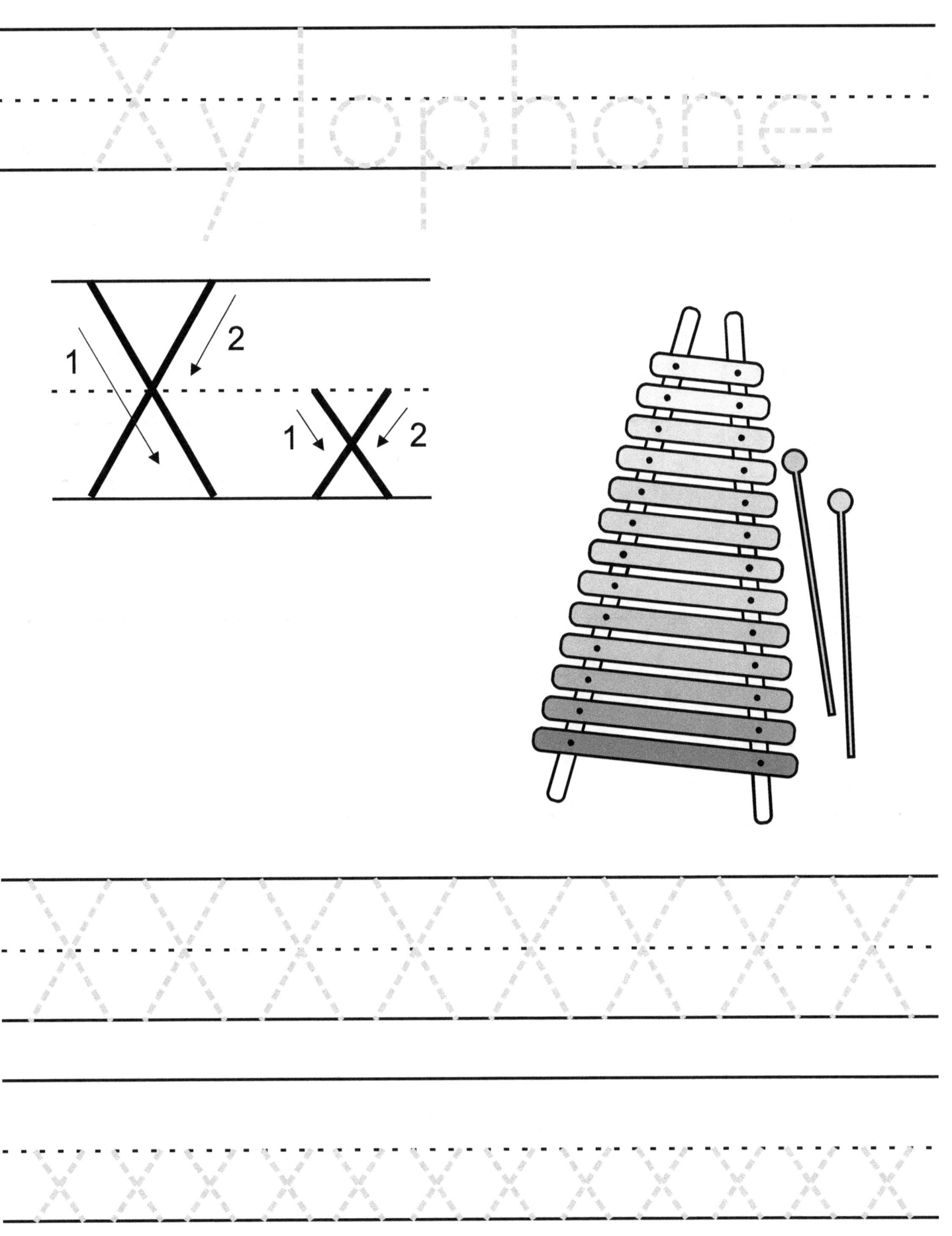

74

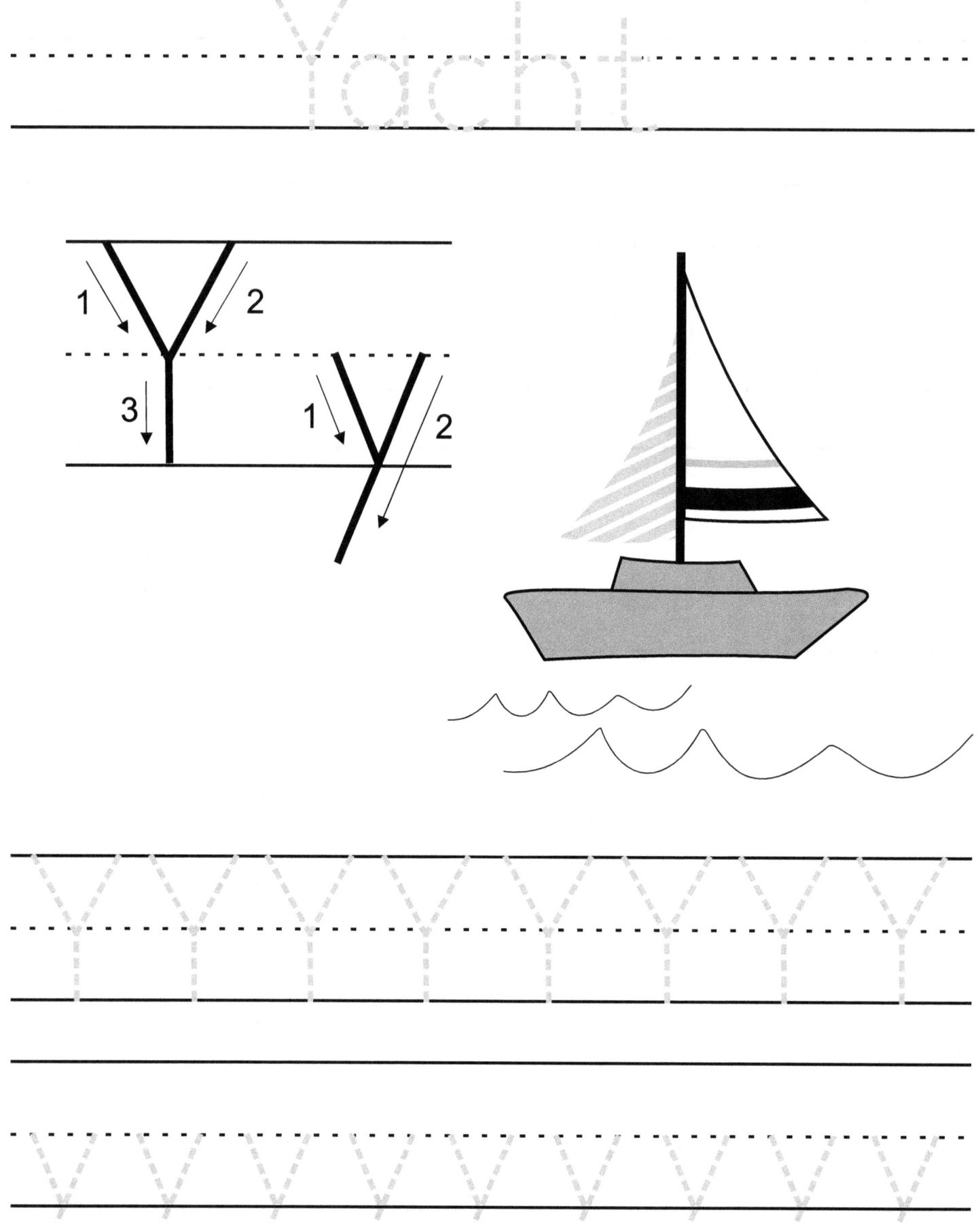

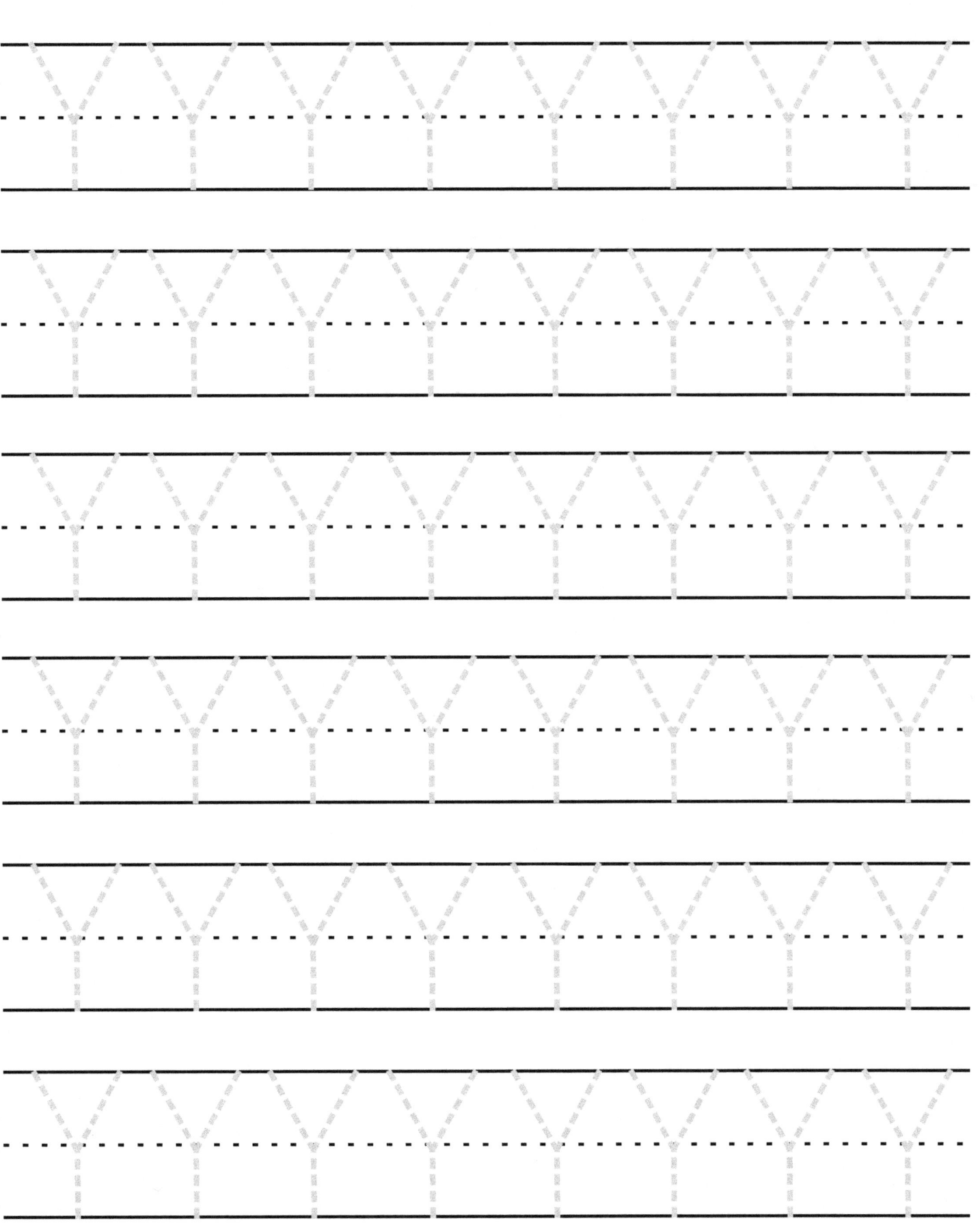

78

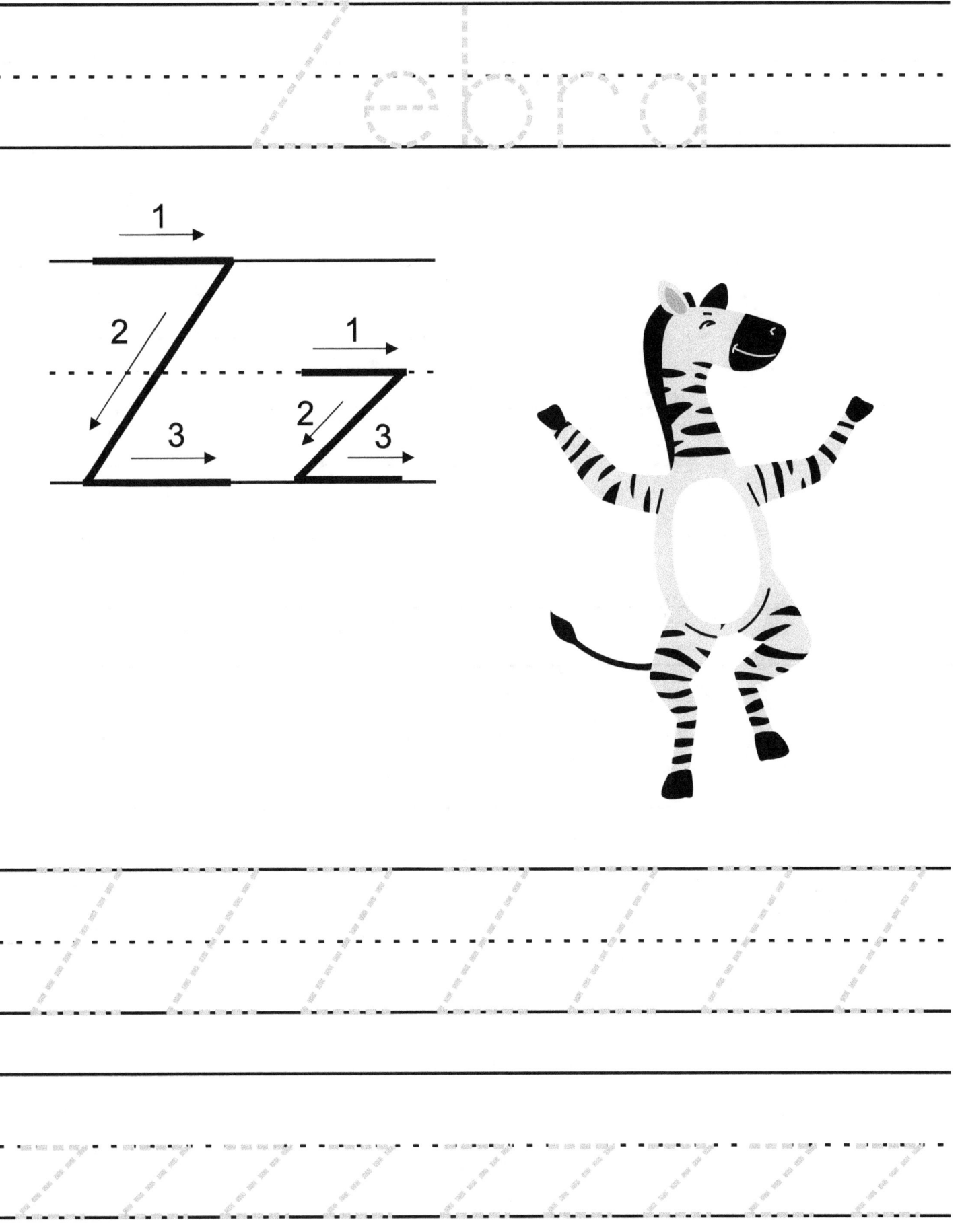

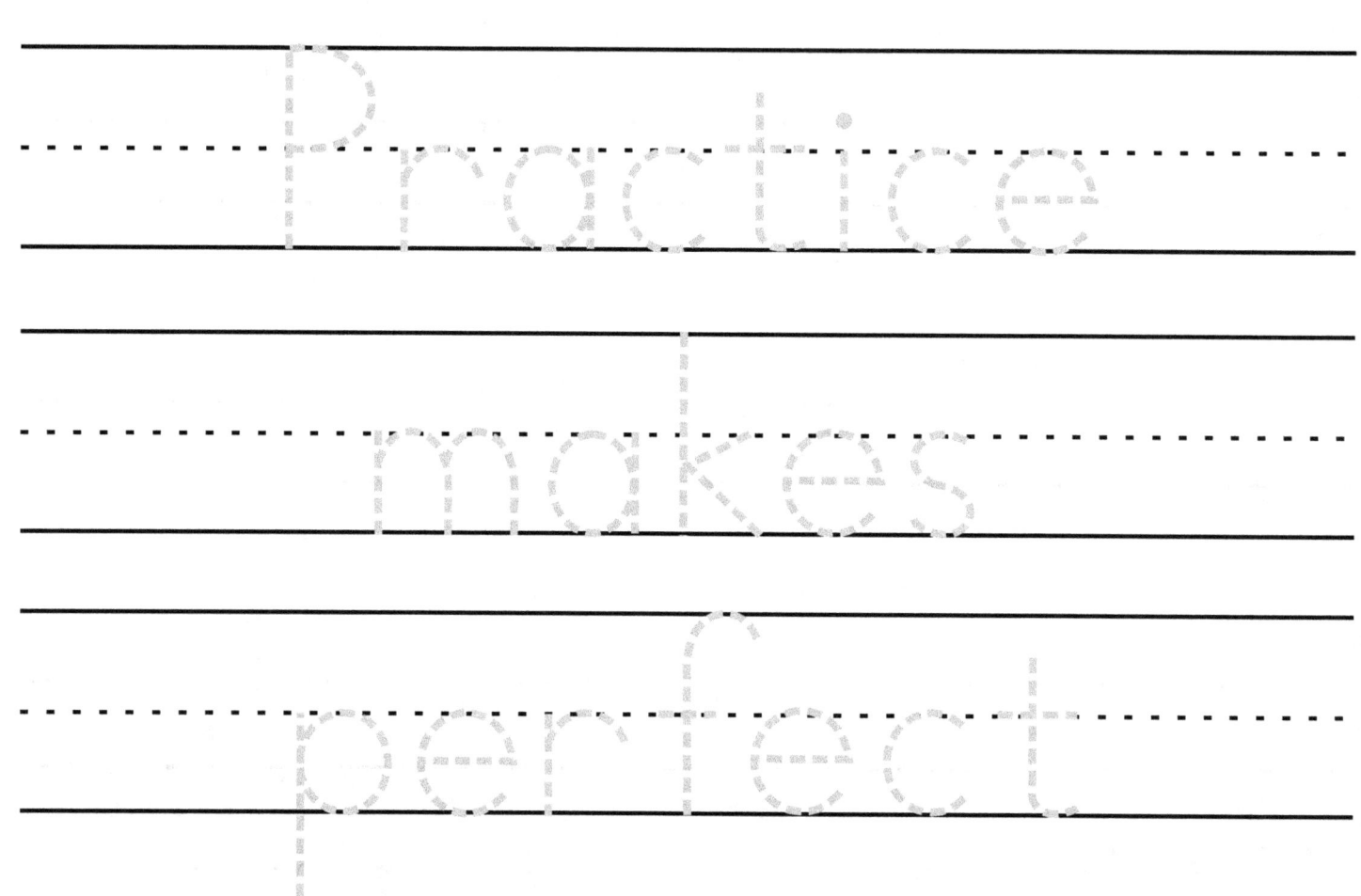

Alligator
Alligator
Alligator
Alligator
Alligator

Butterfly

Butterfly

Butterfly

Butterfly

Butterfly

Cloud Cloud

Cloud Cloud

Cloud Cloud

Cloud Cloud

Cloud Cloud

Dinosaur

Dinosaur

Dinosaur

Dinosaur

Dinosaur

Elephant

Elephant

Elephant

Elephant

Elephant

Fish   Fish

Fish   Fish

Fish   Fish

Fish   Fish

Fish   Fish

Gift Gift
Gift Gift
Gift Gift
Gift Gift
Gift Gift

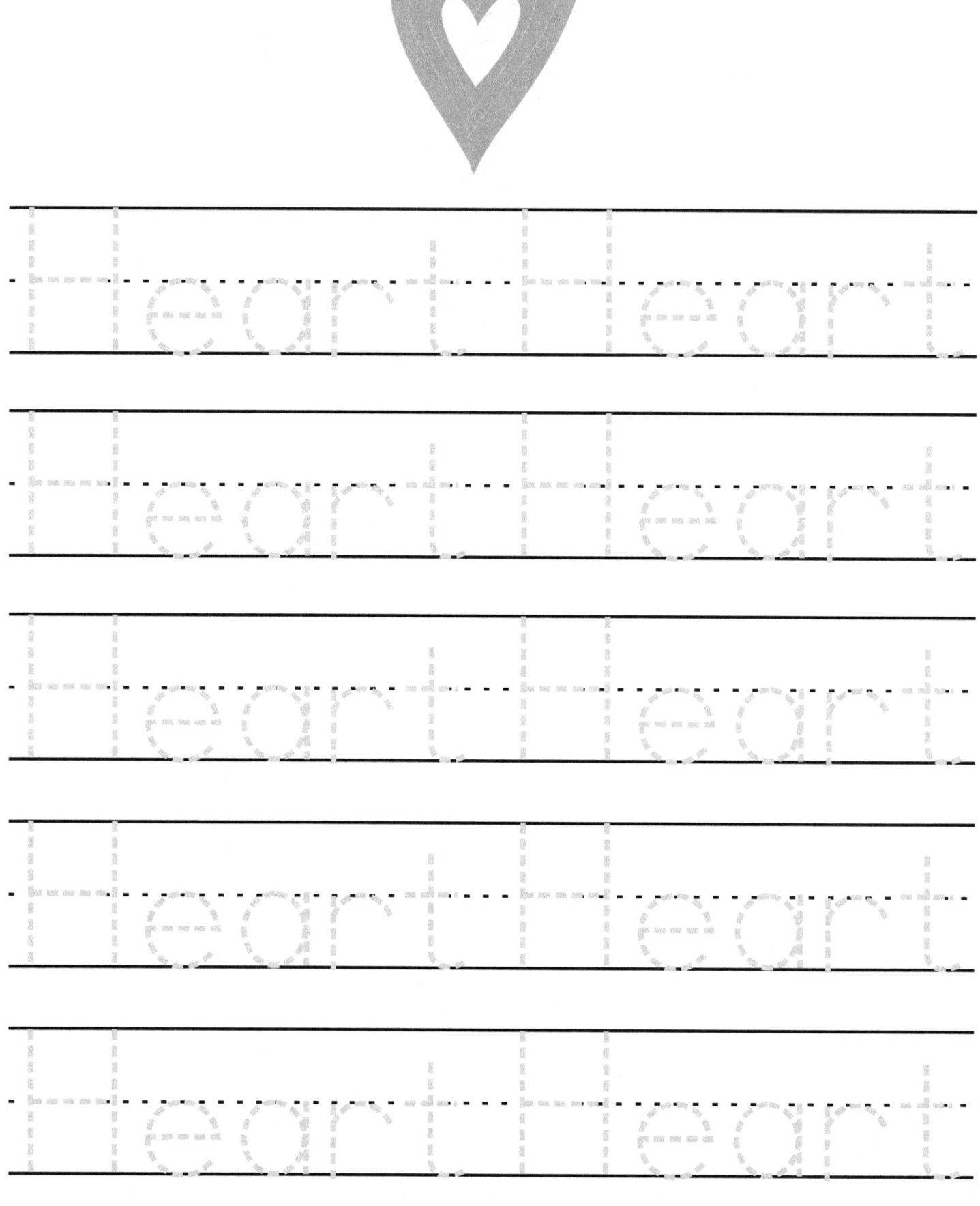

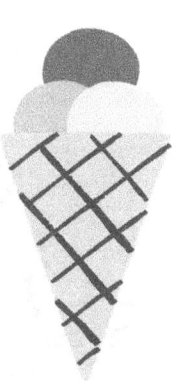

Ice cream

Ice cream

Ice cream

Ice cream

Ice cream

Juice Juice

Juice Juice

Juice Juice

Juice Juice

Juice Juice

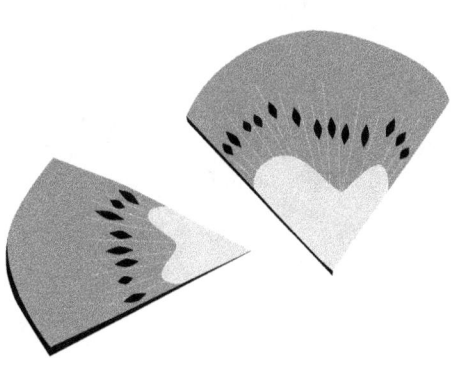

Kiwi Kiwi

Kiwi Kiwi

Kiwi Kiwi

Kiwi Kiwi

Kiwi Kiwi

Leaf Leaf

Leaf Leaf

Leaf Leaf

Leaf Leaf

Leaf Leaf

Money

Money

Money

Money

Money

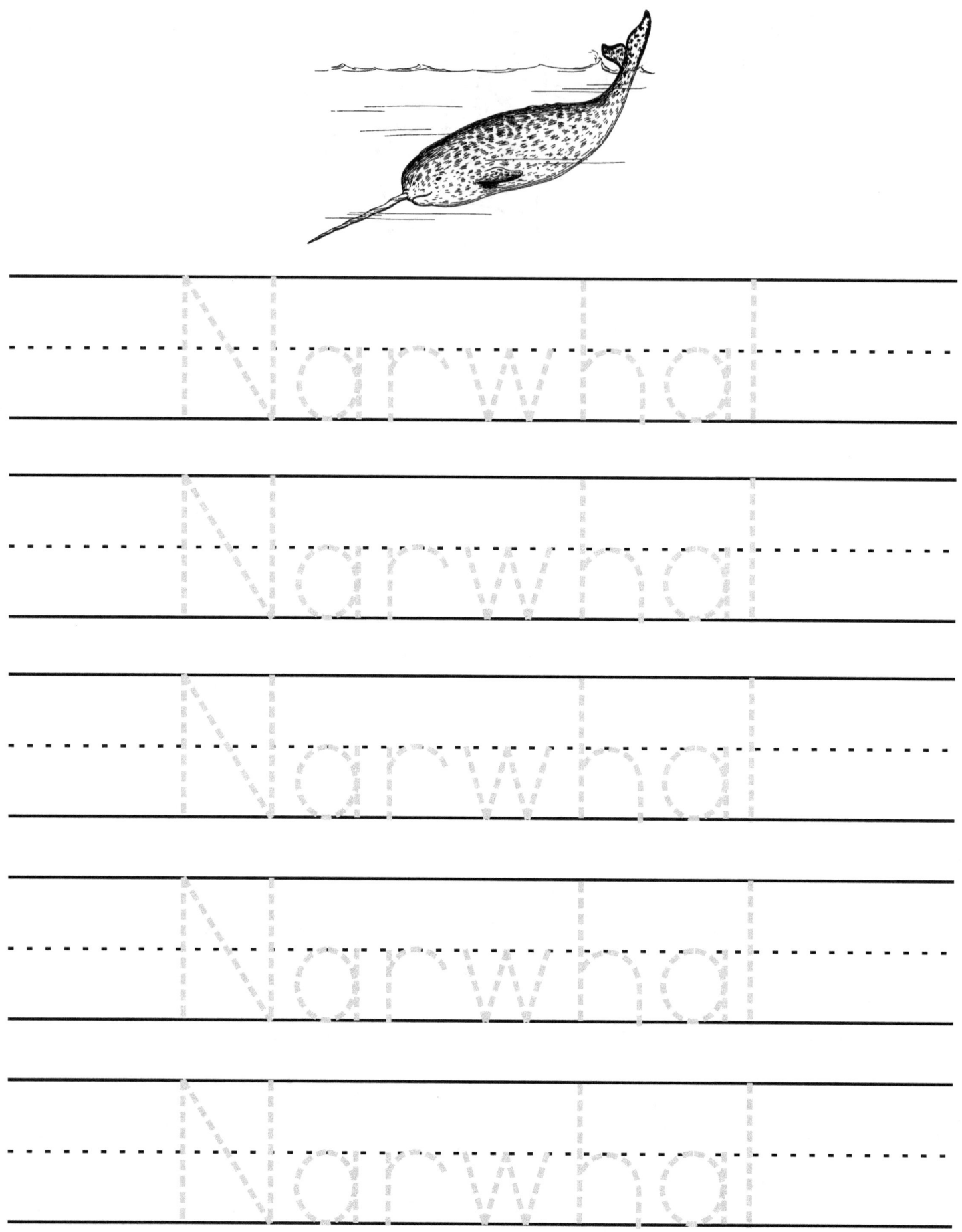

Narwhal

Narwhal

Narwhal

Narwhal

Narwhal

Police Police

Police Police

Police Police

Police Police

Police Police

Quadrant

Quadrant

Quadrant

Quadrant

Quadrant

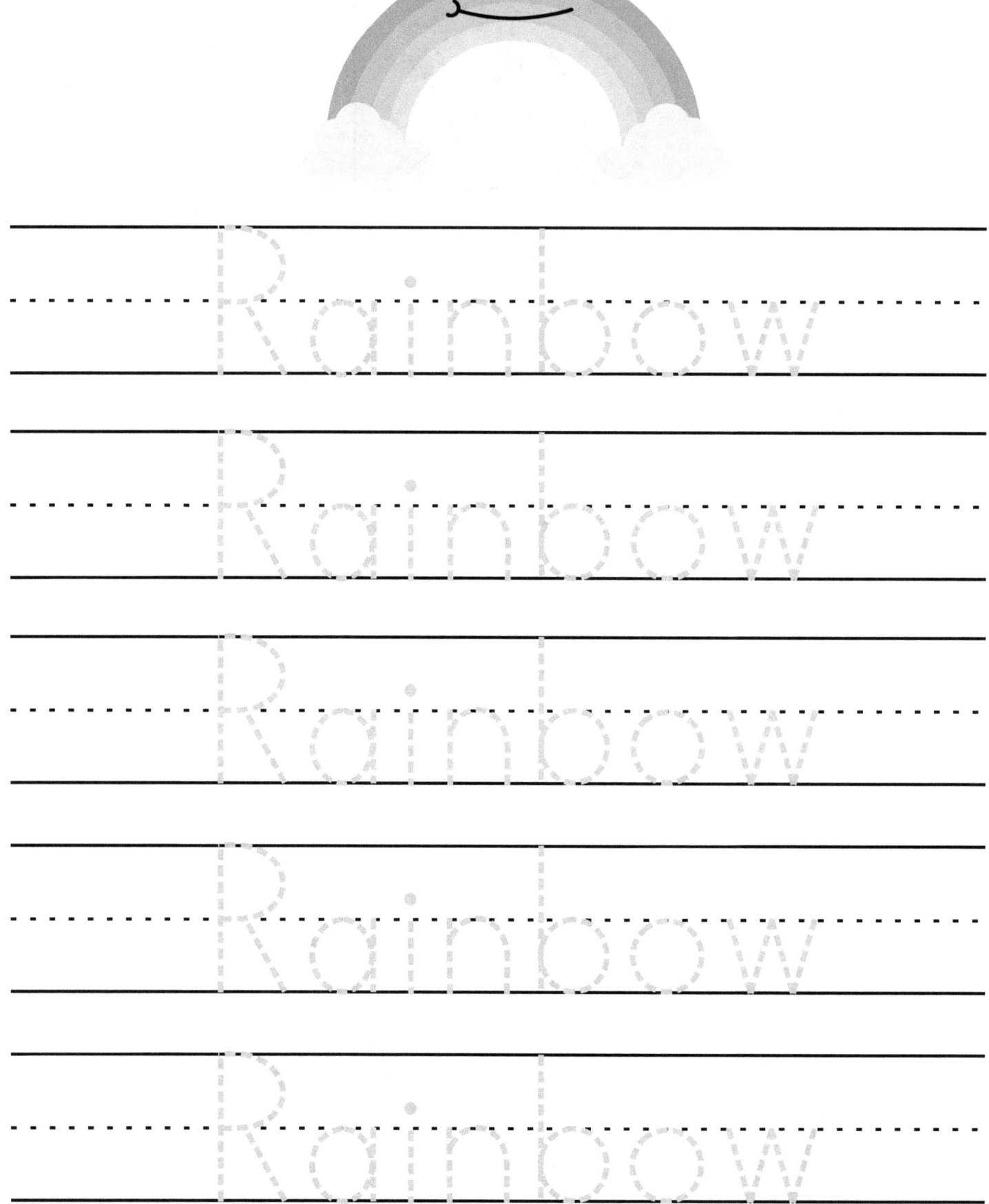

Star Star
Star Star
Star Star
Star Star
Star Star

Unicorn

Unicorn

Unicorn

Unicorn

Unicorn

Volcano

Volcano

Volcano

Volcano

Volcano

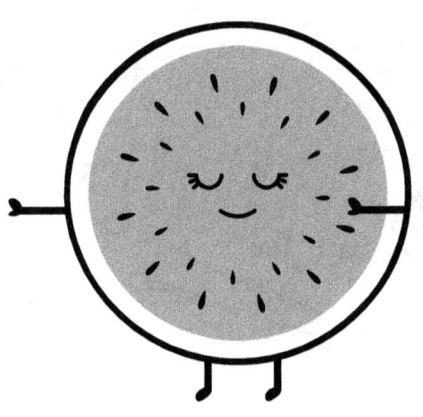

Watermelon

Watermelon

Watermelon

Watermelon

Watermelon

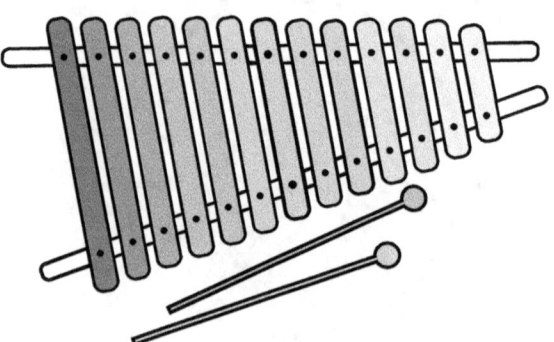

Xylophone
Xylophone
Xylophone
Xylophone
Xylophone

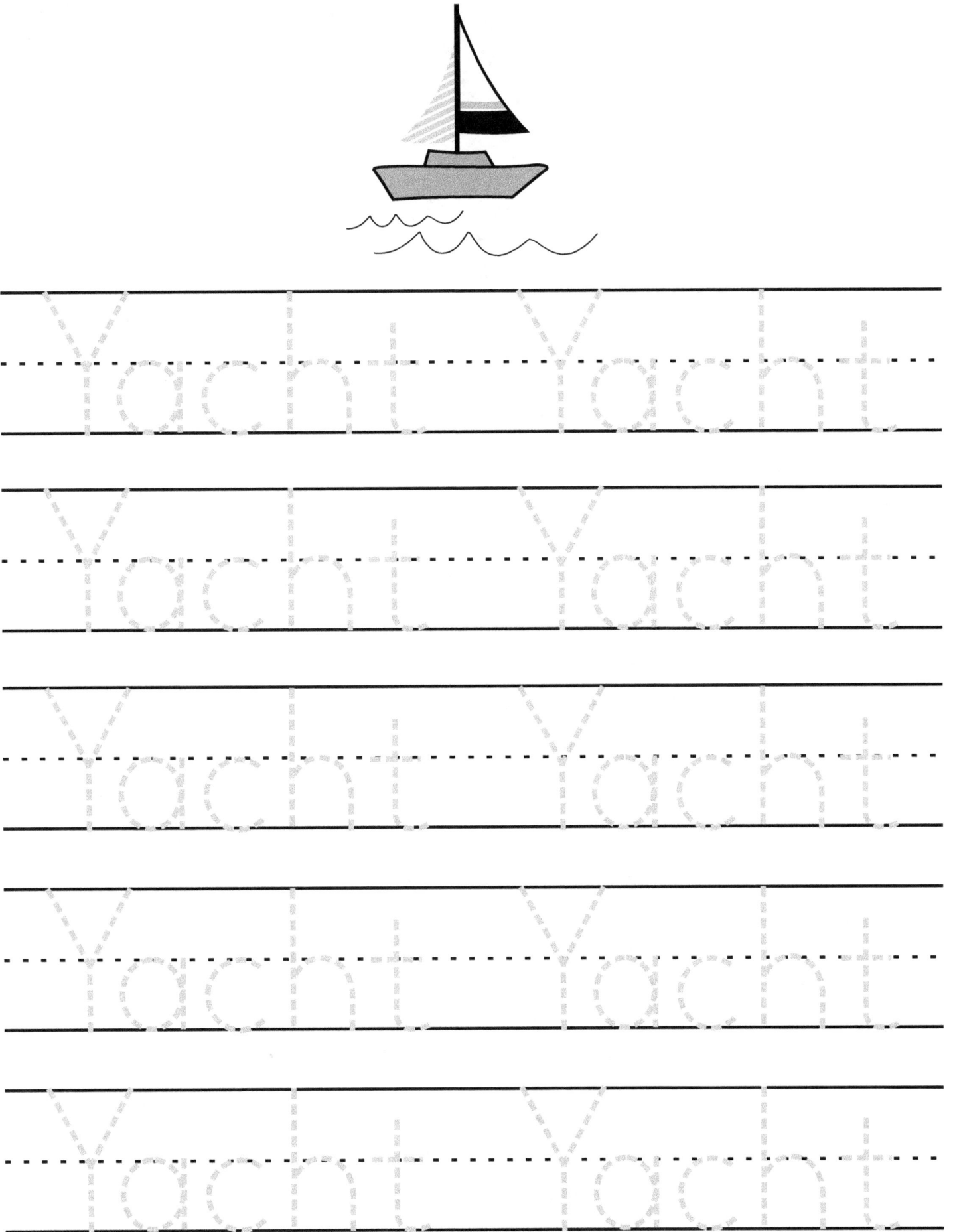

THANK YOU FOR CHOOSING THE "HANDWRITING PRACTICE WORKBOOK" FOR YOUR CHILD. WE'RE THRILLED TO HAVE BEEN A PART OF THEIR LEARNING JOURNEY AND TO SUPPORT THE DEVELOPMENT OF THEIR HANDWRITING SKILLS. WE HOPE THIS WORKBOOK BROUGHT JOY AND NOTICEABLE PROGRESS.

YOUR FEEDBACK IS INCREDIBLY IMPORTANT TO US! IF YOU HAVE A MOMENT, WE'D LOVE TO HEAR YOUR THOUGHTS WHAT YOU LIKED AND WHAT WE COULD IMPROVE TO MAKE OUR PRODUCTS EVEN BETTER AT SUPPORTING CHILDREN'S GROWTH.

WITH WARM REGARDS,
THE "LIFE STYLE DAILY" TEAM